PEOPLE, NATION AND STATE

The Meaning of Ethnicity and Nationalism

Edited by
Edward Mortimer
with Robert Fine

I.B.Tauris *Publishers*
LONDON • NEW YORK

Published in 1999 by I.B.Tauris & Co Ltd
Victoria House, Bloomsbury Square, London WC1B 4DZ
175 Fifth Avenue, New York NY 10010
Website: http://www.ibtauris.com

In the United States and Canada distributed by St. Martin's Press
175 Fifth Avenue, New York NY 10010

ISBN 1 86064 401 5

A full CIP record for this book is available from the British Library
A full CIP record for this book is available from the Library of Congress

Library of Congress catalog card: available

Typeset in Bookman by Dexter Haven, London
Printed and bound in Great Britain by WBC Book Manufacturers, Bridgend

In memory of two great polymaths
and brilliant teachers,
Robert Birley and Ernest Gellner

People, Nation and State

CONTENTS

INTRODUCTION

Edward Mortimer[1]

'What's the strongest political force in Europe today?' The Headmaster's eye glinted. His spectacles swung triumphantly in the air. No-one answered. 'No. Not Marxism. No... It's still nationalism.'

It was certainly a privilege, as a teenager around 1960, to be taught by the late Robert Birley. Not many high school history teachers in any Western country can even have been asking that question at that time, let alone giving that answer. In the 1990s, Birley's observation has become a commonplace. The Soviet Union – whose power, as we can now see, was the main thing that made Marxism seem so important in the middle years of this century – lies in ruins. The relative importance of the part nationalism played in its downfall, as compared to other forces (liberalism, market forces, information technology, etc), will long be debated. What cannot be disputed is the vigour with which nationalism has rushed in to fill the vacuum left by the demise of class-based ideology.

I almost wrote, 'the demise of conflicts based on class and ideology'. But of course, nationalism is also an ideology. It may not recognise itself as such, but then what philosophy does? Remember that, for Marx, ideology meant 'false consciousness'.

What has happened is not the demise of ideology as such, but rather the retreat of universalising ideologies and the triumph of particularising ones.

Samuel Huntington drew attention to this phenomenon in his famous article and subsequent book of the same title, *The Clash of Civilisations?*[2] In the article, he predicted the eventual triumph of Western civilisation, 'or something like it', over all others. In other words, he was still claiming that his own ideas and values were ultimately universalisable. But in the book he retreats into relativism, calling for mutual recognition between different civilisations, which are assimilated to geopolitical blocs, as the best way to avoid conflict. The contradictions in which Huntington has embroiled himself, in his attempt to distil a 'world order' from a thoroughly disorderly world, do not in themselves invalidate his premise. He correctly perceived that, in the aftermath of the Cold War, divisions based on group identity – cultural, ethnic, religious, national – have assumed new importance. It is hard to fill a meeting-hall anywhere these days, let alone a public square, with the cry 'Workers of the world unite!' But in many parts of the world people are being successfully mobilised to defend themselves against real or perceived threats from other groups, whose culture they are encouraged to view as irredeemably alien to their own.

It is true that these conflicts are sometimes between adherents of rival religious orthodoxies, each of which in theory claims universal validity for itself. Yet active proselytising beyond the group already identified with the orthodoxy in question has become exceptional. The emphasis is seldom on the importance of converting 'them' to 'our' point of view. What is stressed is the urgency of defending and strengthening 'our' community or way of life against 'their' aggression or interference or excessive influence. The exponents of such rhetoric seem implicitly to share Huntington's view that humanity is quasi-permanently divided into separate cultural communities.[3]

From Bosnia to Burundi, from California to Kazakhstan, the difficulty of defining and reconciling group identities, and of relating them to state structures, has become one of the central problems of our time. I found it cropping up again and again in my work as a commentator on international affairs for the *Financial Times* from 1987 onwards. It seemed more or less to select itself as the topic I should focus on when, in 1993, I became an honorary professor at the University of Warwick, attached to the Department of Politics and International Studies.

The subject, I knew, was one that had already attracted considerable scholarly attention. For once, indeed, scholarship seems to have been ahead of events. Or, at least, scholars were ahead of journalists and policy-makers in sensing the direction of events. From the early 1980s a series of scholarly works on nationalism had been appearing which, in the words of the author of the most influential among them, 'made largely obsolete the traditional literature on the subject'.[4] I had no pretension to contribute to, or even to summarise, this rich and fascinating body of work, produced by scholars such as Benedict Anderson, Ernest Gellner, Eric Hobsbawm and Anthony Smith. Instead, I conceived the idea of identifying what seemed to me a number of crucial questions, under the general heading of 'ethnicity, nationalism and statehood', and inviting recognised scholars from different fields to debate the answers. This book presents the results of my enquiry.

One of the attractive things about the topic, I found, was that it aroused interest among scholars working in a variety of disciplines – political science, obviously, but also sociology, anthropology, history, philosophy, psychology and law. What proved more difficult than I had expected, however, was to find serious scholars who held clearly opposed views on many of the questions I had selected. Perhaps the field of 'serious scholars' I could tap into was too narrow, or my criteria of seriousness too rigid. More likely, I think, some of the questions which seemed contentious to me, as a layman, are really much less so for people who have studied the subject in depth.

Take the first question, for example: are ethnic identities 'primordial' or are they socially constructed? Outside the academic world, it is a fair bet that 'primordialists' are in the majority. Most people assume, without thinking about it much, that the human race is naturally divided into different races or tribes or nations. They assume that each of these groups is bound together by a common genetic heritage, reinforced by a shared culture, and that such units have existed more or less 'from time immemorial'. These views do not seem to be shared by anyone who has made it their business to study the subject objectively and with academic rigour. But in his contribution to this book, Robin Cohen gamely undertakes a 'modest defence' of a position which is not really his. This has the merit of obliging Terence Ranger to think out and carefully re-state his reasons for rejecting primordialism, and also (as he handsomely acknowledges in the text) to re-think his picture of a 'pre-ethnic Africa'. Contradiction, in other words, proves fruitful, even when somewhat artificial.

My second question was closely related to the first, but transposed the issue from ethnicity to nationhood. Again, there is an almost universally held 'popular' view which holds that nations, even if not literally eternal, do have a long and continuous history reaching well back into the pre-modern era. At least, most Europeans hold that view about their own nations, and usually about neighbouring ones as well. American ideas on the subject are necessarily rather different. The 'founding myth' of American nationalism relates to events in the 18th century, rather than the Dark Ages. Perhaps for that reason, American discourse about other parts of the world often includes the concept of 'nation-building', a term which seems pretentious to the European ear. When one turns to the scholarly literature about nations and nationalism, however, one finds a remarkably solid consensus which holds that these phenomena in their present form are distinctively modern – creatures, roughly, of the last 200 years, and closely related to other new phenomena of that era: mass production, mass education, mass culture. These have transformed the state and rendered necessary a form of identification between it and the mass of its citizens which earlier societies did not know. The 'nations' that we read about in the Bible, or which had their separate colleges in the medieval University of Paris, are therefore quite different from the nation as we conceive or 'imagine' it today.

So far the consensus holds. But there is one quite serious point on which scholars do genuinely disagree. Almost all nationalists trace the origins of their own national identity far back into the pre-modern era.[5] The question is, are they right to do so? Can modern nations be constructed *ex nihilo*, or does there have to be some pre-modern ethnic identity on which to build? On this point, Ernest Gellner took what one might call the radical sceptic view. The issue is, I admit, mis-stated in the title of his contribution here, since Gellner never disputed the reality of nations, still less of nationalism: to deny the reality of a phenomenon which has mobilised millions of people would be either meaningless or absurd.[6] Nor did Gellner deny the importance, as an ingredient in nationalism, of beliefs about the historical continuity of the nation in question. What Gellner thought, and argued with characteristic verve in his speech at Warwick reprinted here (sadly one of the last public appearances of his life), was that the actual veracity or otherwise of these national myths is quite inconsequential. And this is the point on which his former pupil Anthony Smith clearly parts company with him. 'Modern political nationalisms,' Smith argues here, 'cannot be understood without reference to ... earlier ethnic ties and memories, and, in some cases, to pre-modern ethnic identities and communities'. I will not attempt to arbitrate the issue. I simply draw the reader's attention to the fact that there is a real question here, to which each of us must give our own answer.

I thought that there might also be a real question to be debated about gender and nationalism. Confronted with the nationalist phenomenon, the women's movement – it seemed to me – has a choice to make. Either it can repudiate nationalism as a typically phallocratic ideology, or it can seek to reclaim it by documenting the essential but often unsung part that women play in every nationalist movement. (That is one theme that emerges in Linda Colley's classic *Britons: The Making of a Nation.*) Again, however, I reckoned without the sophistication of a serious scholar such as Catherine Hall, whose chapter in this book subsumes and goes beyond both those rather crude (typically male?) perspectives.

My remaining questions all relate in one way or another to the issue of nationalism and democracy. It has long struck me that the connection between these two ideas is closer than most internationalist democrats (a category in which I should like to count myself) feel comfortable with. Not that all nationalists are democrats or all nation-states are democratically governed. Obviously not. But the essential premises of nationalism and democracy are closely related: the notion that the people precedes the state and that the state belongs to it. In much of the literature, especially in the seminal period of the French Revolution, the words 'people' and 'nation' are used interchangeably. And the connection does not stop there. Democracy, by giving power to the majority of citizens, gives questions of culture and community an urgency which they do not have so long as power is legitimised by dynastic or religious arguments. If decisions that may affect my most vital interests are to be taken by a majority of my fellow-citizens, I need to feel a great deal of confidence in them. I may not mind being on the losing side in an election once in a while, or even every time, so long as the issues on which elections are fought do not threaten my existence or call my identity into question; so long, in other words, as I feel confident that majority and minority together form a single community with shared perceptions and interests. But democracy has little to offer me if I feel that I and people like me are permanently and structurally in a minority. In that case, I may feel obliged to choose between assimilation – effectively, changing my identity in order to identify with the majority – and secession, which means declaring (first to myself, then to fellow members of my own minority community, and finally, most dangerously, to the world at large) that I do not belong to this electorate because the majority is composed of people whose identity I do not share and who therefore cannot legitimately claim to represent me.

Three pairs of chapters in this book look at this problem from different angles, and at possible solutions. In the first pair, the question posed is: what degree of common culture or shared values is needed for people to live together in a democratically-governed state? Mischievously, I posed this question under the heading 'multiculturalism versus laicité', and invited a French specialist on Islam, Olivier Roy, to debate it with a noted British expert on community relations, Bhikhu Parekh. Once again, the two positions turn out to be less straightforwardly antithetical than one might suppose, but the difference of perspective, derived from different national experience, produces a rich dialogue which is certainly enlightening to the reader, and I think was also to the protagonists.

Parekh is not an extreme or stereotypical multiculturalist. He does not deny the need for certain common values, or even a common culture, to underpin democratic practice. But he argues that a distinction must be made between the common political culture, required for the stability and cohesion of any democratic state, and the different 'ways of life' which can and must coexist in a multicultural society. The biggest danger, as he sees it, arises from attempts by a dominant ethnic group, arguing from its majority status or from its historical association with the state and territory in question, to claim ownership of the political culture and to identify it with aspects of its own way of life, which then become 'loyalty tests' imposed on other communities, often with the effect of excluding them, or making them feel excluded, from the democratic polity. Norman Tebbit's famous complaint about minorities in the UK applauding the 'wrong' cricket team would be an extreme example – perhaps a *reductio ad absurdum* – of this danger.

Similarly Olivier Roy is not a caricature apologist for French Jacobinism , seeking to impose a uniform civic culture or to confine all expressions of communal or religious identity to the purely private sphere. But – rightly, in my view – he does point out the threat to individual freedom which can arise from attempts to institutionalise multiculturalism. The law, he argues 'should not define any category which a citizen is supposed to belong to, by nature, birth, culture or by a tentative choice which would be difficult to rescind'.[7]

If we accept that some minimum degree of community is necessary to make democracy feasible, a further question inevitably arises sooner or later, namely what are the criteria for deciding, and who has the right to decide, whether a given group of people possesses that degree of community or not? This, of course, is the classic issue of national self-determination. It more commonly arises in negative form: who decides whether a given group of people has such a specific separate communal identity that its members cannot be considered free so long as they have to coexist in the same polity as a larger group?

This was the question I posed to the next pair of contributors: an outstanding theorist and practitioner of international law, and a leading academic authority on international relations. The former, Danilo Türk, played an important role in a specific act of national self-determination, when his country, Slovenia, declared itself independent in June 1991, thereby initiating the formal dissolution of the Yugoslav Federation. (Appropriately enough, he now represents Slovenia at the United Nations.) In his contribution here he examines the current state of international law on self-determination, and particularly on the recognition of new states by the international community. He looks at three types of objective criteria which have been suggested.

The first of these is the liberal, which essentially give 'a people' the right to opt out of a state where it no longer feels at home. This doctrine is generally faulted on two grounds. First, it begs the question it is meant to solve, namely what constitutes a people. Secondly, the interests of the seceding 'people' are not the only ones affected. Others should be allowed a say in the matter. Türk concedes this, but suggests that the argument should cut both ways: if no people has an absolute right to secede, nor should any people have an absolute right to hold another indefinitely in a union to which it does not consent. (A similarly balanced conclusion was reached by the Supreme Court of Canada, in its recent decision on the right of Quebec to secede.)

The second is the criterion of 'self-preservation', which allows a people to claim independent statehood when threatened with annihilation.

The last is those involving a more 'comprehensive political calculation', which takes into account such factors as the legitimacy of the claim that 'the people' is constituted as such, the representative character of the government claiming statehood in the name of 'the people', and the degree of destabilisation the claim entails.

Türk finds none of these approaches entirely satisfactory. He concludes that 'a certain level of subjective political judgement will continue to be necessary'. That suggests that, in practice, might will continue to be the better part of right, and the price of statehood will continue, in most cases, to be conflict and bloodshed.

Such a conclusion fits well with Adam Roberts's careful and sceptical, not to say magisterial, dissection of the whole concept of national self-determination. Roberts rightly warns against any attempt to be too tidy or systematic in organising the relationship between nations and states. He suggests that 'self-determination should be stripped of the word "national" and become a more open-ended concept'; that 'views of the character and function of the state need to change'; and that 'there should be more open acceptance of the possibility of variations, ambiguities and anomalies in the status of many territories'. Thus Roberts implicitly declares my question 'who has the right to decide?' unanswerable, and instead answers my next question, 'Do you need a state?' in the negative. He warns against making the leap from communal to national identity (because the latter in most contexts entails an implicit if not explicit demand for statehood), and urges that ways of expressing communal identity other than through separate statehood be explored.

This is precisely the theme which Gidon Gottlieb develops in the following chapter, summarising the argument of his book *Nation Against State*.[8] He calls for 'fresh thinking about functional territorial arrangements in disputed lands', as well as 'new sets of concepts in regard to borders, national homes, citizenship, nationality and forms of association between peoples'.

Gottlieb denounces the two 'pernicious doctrines' that 'national sovereignty must be absolute' and that 'in every state there must be one nation'. The time has come, he argues, 'to come up with new constitutional and doctrinal frameworks to conciliate between the notion of absolute sovereignty and state unity and between national rights and claims for separation which threaten states whose integrity is a pillar of international peace'. Thus some 'national rights' could cut across state borders, without breaking up existing states. The Good Friday agreement in Northern Ireland, negotiated since Gottlieb's chapter was written, provides an example of the kind of arrangements he had in mind.

To debate with Gottlieb I invited Neil MacCormick, who besides being Regius Professor of Law at Edinburgh is a leading light in the Scottish National Party. That party advocates the dissolution of the United Kingdom in order to re-establish the Scottish national state which was merged with England in 1707. I therefore hoped MacCormick would insist on the right of every nation to its own state, but in this I was disappointed. MacCormick does indeed favour 'independence in Europe' for Scotland (the SNP's slogan), but only because he thinks the European Union offers a less problematic way of 'continuing union among the parts of the British Isles' than the awkward not-quite-federal form of Scottish autonomy which is now in the process of being implemented. He is not prepared to make this the basis of a general disagreement with Gottlieb's approach – arguing, on the contrary, that it is compatible with the spirit of that approach. On the general point, MacCormick agrees with

Gottlieb in preferring 'liberal nationalism' to 'sovereign-state nationalism'. He is a classic liberal in that he gives priority to the autonomy of the individual, but argues that 'a sense of national identity and belonging does for a very large part of the present population of the world play an important part in individuals' self-understanding'. Individuals see themselves as members of a nation, and as such are 'in principle entitled to effective organs of political self-government within the world order of sovereign or post-sovereign states'.

But, he goes on, this principle has to be implemented in ways that do not conflict with other 'equally important, or more important, values and principles'. It is also subject to 'constraints of time, place and circumstance'. Therefore, while each nation is entitled to organs of self-government, 'these need not provide for self-government in the form of a sovereign state'.

Looking back over my questions, then, it will be seen that: there is no real disagreement on the socially constructed (as opposed to 'primordial') nature of ethnicity; there is no disagreement on either the 'reality' or the specifically modern character of nations and nationalism as we know them today, but there is a vigorous and entertaining debate on the narrower issue of whether modern nations do or do not need any real continuity with pre-modern ethnic groups; there is no real debate about the relationship between nationalism and gender, although mainstream scholarship puts less emphasis on this relationship than does a feminist writer like Catherine Hall.

There is, if not exactly a debate, at any rate a clear difference of emphasis on the degree of common culture and values needed to sustain a democratic polity, and on the wisdom of giving official recognition to communal or cultural categories within such a polity. There is no real dispute about the difficulty and danger of basing claims to statehood on the 'right of national self-determination' but, again, a difference of emphasis. Türk places more emphasis than Roberts on the opposite danger of meeting such claims with a blank refusal. There is no argument for an absolute correlation between self-perceived national identity and sovereign statehood, but a consensus on the need for pragmatism and imagination in finding other ways for such identities to express themselves when sovereign statehood seems likely to entail infringement of the rights of other groups, or a threat to civil or international peace.

It was my final question – is there such a thing as benign nationalism? – which provoked the most genuine debate. I was on fairly safe ground here, because one of the protagonists had already taken issue with the other, in print, before I solicited their views. In an article in *Democratization* (Autumn 1994),

Robert Fine had criticised Michael Ignatieff, along with Julia Kristeva and Jürgen Habermas, for making too neat a distinction between 'civic nationalism' (good) and 'ethnic nationalism' (bad).

The contributions of Fine and Ignatieff in this book do reveal a certain amount of common ground, but their positions remain clearly distinct and opposed to each other. Ignatieff concedes that 'civic' doesn't necessarily mean 'benign', and that '"civic" language can be turned against dissidents and minorities just as "ethnic" language can'. He remains convinced, however, both that nationalism can be benign, and that it can only become so if it 'becomes truly civic'. He rejects 'cosmopolitanism' as being 'the privilege of those who can take their own membership in secure nation-states for granted', although a very similar observation about 'patriotism' is apparently not sufficient grounds for rejecting it.

While Ignatieff believes that civic nationalism cannot afford to maintain national cohesion by tapping ethnically-based emotions ('common tradition, national story, shared ethnicity, food, culture') because most modern democracies now contain ethnic minorities whom such references will serve to exclude rather than include, Fine carries the argument a stage further. He fears that relying on any form of nationalism to make social cohesion or civility more persuasive runs the risk of elevating prejudice and enthusiasm at the expense of reason, and may be a dangerous substitute for addressing the social concerns of the less privileged members of society. Fine questions the over-hasty pathologising of 'ethnic nationalism' from the civic nationalist perspective, and turns the gaze around to explore how 'civic nationalism' looks from the ethnic perspective. He stresses the family resemblance between the 'civic' and 'ethnic' forms of nationalism, and looks instead to the nurturing of social solidarities across national as well as ethnic boundaries: to cultures of 'national civility informing everyday social relations between individuals... rather than to cultures which focus on flags, anthems and parades'. However, he also cautions against the absolute devaluation of nationalism or the elevation of cosmopolitanism as its unequivocal antidote. This latter project may be no more unrealistic than Ignatieff's aspiration to draw the fangs of nationalism and render it benign, but Fine leaves the reader with the uneasy fear that both projects may be ill-fated.

The relationship between ethnicity, national identity and state sovereignty continues to provoke passionate debate almost everywhere, from multiculturalism in the US to self-determination in East Timor. This book does not pretend to resolve such issues, but I hope it does something to clarify them.

NOTES ON INTRODUCTION

1 My thanks are due to all at the University of Warwick who helped plan and organise the debates from which this book is derived, and especially to Barbara Allen Roberson, whose idea it was to invite me to Warwick in the first place, and to Robert Fine, who undertook the work of editing and preparing the text for publication.
2 Samuel P. Huntington, 'The Clash of Civilisations?', *Foreign Affairs*, Summer 1993; Samuel P. Huntington, *The Clash of Civilisations and the Remaking of World Order* (New York: Simon & Schuster, 1996).
3 Indeed Huntington resembles them in his anxiety that the United States may destroy itself by renouncing its Western identity and becoming multicultural: Huntington, *The Clash of Civilisations and the Remaking of World Order*, *op. cit.*, pp 305–6.)]
4 Benedict Anderson, *Imagined Communities* (London, Verso, 1991), p xii. The comment refers to the work of other scholars, but certainly applies to Anderson's own.
5 The Americans, as already noted, are the most conspicuous exception. But traditional American historiography largely appropriates English history before the eighteenth century as a kind of pre-history of the American nation. The desire of 'multiculturalists' to dilute this with parallel pre-histories for other ethnic components of present-day America must partly explain why Huntington and his ilk see multiculturalism as a threat to their national identity.
6 Nor did Anderson, with his brilliant title *Imagined Communities*, ever mean to suggest that modern nations are imaginary!
7 A similar point is made fictionally by Steven Lukes in the chapter on 'Communitaria' in his delightful satirical novel *The Curious Enlightenment of Professor Caritat*.
8 Gidon Gottlieb, *Nation Against State* (New York: Council on Foreign Relations, 1993).

PART I

ETHNICITY

1

THE MAKING OF ETHNICITY: A MODEST DEFENCE OF PRIMORDIALISM

Robin Cohen[1]

In 1908, an American playwright, Israel Zangwill, wrote a Broadway hit called *The Melting Pot*. In his play, one of the characters, a refugee from the pogroms of Eastern Europe, makes this impassioned speech:

> America is God's crucible, the great melting pot where all the races of Europe are melting and reforming! Here you stand, good folk, think I, when I see them at Ellis Island, here you stand in your fifty groups with your fifty languages and histories, and your fifty blood hatreds and rivalries, but you won't be long like that brothers, for these are the fires of God you've come to – these are the fires of God. A fig for your feuds and vendettas! Germans and Frenchmen, Irishmen and Englishmen, Jews and Russians – into the crucible with you all. God is making the American.[2]

The expression 'the melting pot' subsequently became a slogan for all those who believed that civic nationalism, or modernisation, or education, or class allegiances, or better communications, would dissolve prior ethnic loyalties. Three generations on from the staging of Zangwill's play, and we still have to ask the question 'why does ethnicity not dissolve in the melting pot?' Croats and Serbs in the Balkans, Hutu and Tutsi in Rwanda, Christians and Muslims in Lebanon, Jews and Arabs in the Middle East, Tamils and Sinhalese in Sri Lanka, Protestants and Catholics in Northern Ireland – all these examples and many more show the persistence, tenacity or re-emergence of ethnic differences.

For the racist, the answer is obvious. We have been endowed by the force of nature with different biological imprints. 'Races' regard each other with apprehension, suspicion and hatred because, the race theorists say, we have different genetic make-ups and different God-given destinies. We can immediately recognise some of the absurdities of this argument. Until they begin to hurl insults at each other, the Tutsi and Hutu cannot tell each other apart, Jews and Arabs are both of Semitic descent, Protestants and Catholics in Northern Ireland are evidently not of different races. Where there are differences in appearance, biblical and divine authority – as in the story of the dispersal of Noah's sons to the far corners of the earth – are implausibly used to explain the diversity of the species.

Racial myths and biblical quotes are clearly insufficient to explain the endurance of ethnicity. Probably the most heated, but none the less suggestive, debate between scholars on this question has been the conflict between the 'primordialists' and the so-called 'social constructionists'. It would be difficult for any contemporary scholar to defend a primordialist case *tout court*, and I do not propose to do so here. Yet the very vehemence of the anti-primordialist attacks attract a certain suspicion.[3] Their almost exclusive targets comprise a deceased social and political theorist, Edward Shils, whose article on the issue was published in 1957, and a retired anthropologist, Clifford Geertz, who expressed his views in a 1963 essay published in a book ten years later.[4]

What were the primordialists arguing? As Geertz and Shils make clear, they regard primordial sentiments as just one form of identity among others (personal, sacred, civic, etc). They do, nonetheless, suggest that there is a core identity that is logically and emotionally prior to any other forms of identity. It is so fundamental and so basic because it has to do with psychological necessity and even the instinct for survival. Let me quote Geertz himself:

> By a *primordial* attachment is meant one that stems from the 'givens' of social existence... congruities of blood, speech, custom, and so on, *are seen* to have an ineffable, and at times overpowering, coerciveness in and of themselves. One is bound to one's kinsman, one's neighbour, one's fellow believer, *ipso facto* [by that very fact]; as the result not merely of personal affection, practical necessity, common interest, or incurred obligation, but at least in great part by virtue of some unaccountable absolute import attributed to the very tie itself [emphasis added].[5]

The expression 'congruities of blood' derives from largely discredited racist musings, but Geertz's argument is not by any means as crude, or as easy to refute, as it might appear. The crucial phrase is that common blood, kinship, belief, etc 'are seen' to be primordial.

I shall come back to this question of perception later, but I want to make my own position clear. I would accept that primordialism does not work well as an explanation of ethnic difference, but it certainly works as a description of the extraordinary force that is contained in ethnic sentiment. For many people, ethnic ties are a matter of loyalty, of pride, of location, of belonging, of refuge, of identity, trust, acceptance and security. It is the type of attachment that most parents feel for their children and most siblings feel for one another. As Anton Allahar suggests, such ties imply an unquestioned affinity and devotion purely on the basis of the intimacy of the tie. It is the closest form of association that can be achieved by a collectivity of humans. It expresses their gregariousness and preference for group membership rather than the social rejection of a misfit or the isolation of a hermit. By embracing an ethnic identity, groups of human beings acknowledge that they are parts of society, that their survival depends on forces bigger than the individual, that the locality into which they were born and which has nurtured them is an object of affection – and that there are others who share their origin and their likely fate.[6]

THREE ATTACKS ON ETHNICITY

I have said enough, I think, to show how important ethnic bonds are in the lives of most people. That is what makes ethnicity so powerful – and also potentially so destructive. Partly because of its destructive capacity, and for other reasons too, ethnicity has been under attack from at least three quarters.

First, Marxists sought to abolish ethnicity as merely an epiphenomenon or as an instance of false consciousness. For Marxists the only form of true consciousness was class consciousness. But while class may indeed be a powerful form of association, powerful enough sometimes to rival or overdetermine ethnic consciousness, it makes no particular sense to call the one 'true' and dismiss the other as 'false' consciousness. Class consciousness arises, as Marx averred, from an objectively different relationship to the means of production, distribution and exchange shared by those who sell their labour power, own capital or trade in commodities or services. These different positions give them different interests. As is now generally accepted, contemporary capitalism has produced conditions whereby these interests become conflated and diluted. However, a more fundamental critique of the idea of class consciousness as the only true consciousness is that class awareness is predominantly an awareness of interest. And despite the beliefs of Marxists and free-marketeers alike, people live not just by interests alone but also by their emotions. They live by anger, grief, anxiety, jealousy, affection, fear and devotion.

Second, ethnicity has also been under attack from rulers of nation-states. I am talking of course of that type of nation-state which contains within its territory people of different ethnic origin who are asked to subordinate that origin in the interests of the nation as a whole. Unlike the case of class, the nation is offered as an object of affection, not merely as a vehicle for advancing an interest. One is enjoined to love one's country, to revere its institutions, to salute its flag, to support its sporting teams, to fight and die for it in war. In these claims, the nation is a rival form of identification to the ethnic group and again, as in class consciousness, it is powerful enough sometimes to rival or overdetermine ethnic consciousness. But the nation-state is often too large and too amorphous an entity to be the object of intimate affection. One can marry a spouse of one's own kind and feel the warm embrace of kinship; one can kneel in common prayer with one's co-religionists; one can effect easier friendships with those of a common background; one can eat one's own ethnic cuisine and, in a sense, ingest one's ethnicity (an idea conveyed in the reference by African Americans to 'soul food'). The nation-state cannot easily rival these attachments.

Thirdly, ethnicity is under attack from those who see it as an irrelevant anachronism in the face of the gathering pace of globalisation. It is true that we are becoming increasingly interdependent in economic and cultural terms, that there is an increased awareness that we are 'one world' facing common ecological, political and security problems. Yet this very process of globalisation, the very rapidity of the dissolution of the known world, creates a perverse effect. People reach out to the habitual, to the communities where they find familiar faces, voices, sounds, smells, tastes and places. Confronted by the pace of globalisation they often need ethnicity more not less. Confused by post-modernity, relativism and the deconstruction of their known world, they reaffirm and reify what they believe to be true at a more local level.[7]

I am suggesting in these observations that ethnicity is a much more powerful force than many of us would, perhaps, like to accept, and that ethnicity does not disappear when confronted with the rival claims of class interest, or the demands of nation-building, or the impelling force of globalisation.

HOW ETHNICITY ARISES: THREE OBJECTIVE FACTORS

Even if we accept that ethnicity is an uncomfortably powerful force, how do we explain how ethnic differences arise? Typically, social constructionists exaggerate the element of individual choice and underplay the extent to which objective factors cause and help to perpetuate ethnic differences. Let me allude to just three ways in which ethnicity can be moulded by objective forces.

First, in many settings there were legal and political restrictions on what occupations and activities were permitted to subordinated groups. I shall give just one, admittedly extreme, example. Until the end of legal apartheid in South Africa in 1989, blacks, whites, coloureds and Asians were legally separated from one another, while the black section of the population was subdivided into ethnicities – Zulu, Tswana, Xhosa etc. While we can all recognise the artificiality of a number of these distinctions, the argument has to be pressed one stage further. Legal distinctions were given force in economic, educational and occupational terms and determined the limits of opportunity in terms of access to good housing or health care. Ethnic identities were, in short, not selected but imposed by law and the threat of state violence.

Second, ethnic differences arose through various kinds of coerced migration. Colonial and mercantile powers often brought different peoples to new settings for work on their plantations or to further their commercial interests: for example, ten million African slaves were transhipped across the Atlantic; 1.4 million Indian indentured workers were sent to the sugar plantations; the Governor of Dutch Indonesia sent warships to capture Chinese on the mainland, and blockaded the port of Manila so that Chinese traders would help to develop his colony. These patterns of involuntary migration led to complex, often three–way, interactions as indigenous people faced outsiders, who faced other outsiders, who all faced representatives of the colonial powers. Alluding to the time and circumstances in which immigrants were brought in, some social theorists developed a helpful concept of 'differential incorporation' which shows how occupational categories fused with ethnic identities. Thus, we have an evolution of a sort of paired 'ethno-class', a phenomenon evoked by these familiar descriptions: 'Chinese traders',

'Indian 'coolies', 'Sikh soldiers', 'Irish navvies', 'Lebanese middlemen', 'Scottish engineers' etc.

A third objective factor which limits the way in way in which ethnicity is socially constructed is the one that is obvious, yet uncomfortable to state. Quite often peoples look rather different to one another. In popular language they are white, brown, black or yellow, dark or light skinned, Nordic, Mediterranean, Latin American or Asian-looking. Of course, these are absurdly unscientific categories, and of course I recognise that the human species overwhelmingly shares a common set of characteristics and traits. To provide a limited defence for primordialism is not to accept any ridiculous exercise in racial typologies. Rather I want simply to affirm that appearance – technically phenotype – can provide constraints to how far one can imagine oneself into another ethnicity. There are, in other words, real limits to the manipulative use of identity changes. It is relatively easy to change one's religion or one's clothes. It is less easy to change one's accent, manner and language, though Ms Doolittle managed to do it with considerable success in G.B. Shaw's *Pygmalion*. It is very difficult to alter one's physical appearance, one's phenotype. In my imagination, I have always rather fancied the idea of being a Masai warrior, but I would make a rather implausible mess of it if I tried to convince a real Masai warrior that I was just like him.

I have discussed only three kinds of exogenous pressures that serve to create or perpetuate ethnic differences – legal and political restrictions, the consequences of coerced migration, and phenotypical appearances. But the implication is clear. Ethnic differences are often compelled – or at least strongly induced – and are only in a limited way chosen. Individuals cannot attach themselves to, or withdraw from, any ethnicity at will. The idea that an individual constructs and presents any one of a number of possible social identities, depending on the situation, is clearly an exaggeration.

HOW ETHNICITY ARISES: SUBJECTIVE ELEMENTS

So far I have suggested that primordialism provides a good description of the power of ethnic sentiment, but that we can better explain ethnic differences through objective historical and sociological data. However, I do not want to neglect the subjective elements in the making and sustaining of ethnic consciousness. It is time now to turn to the question of perception, which I flagged earlier. For the primordialists, the subjective dimension turns on the question of the meaning of ethnicity to the actors themselves. Ethnic differences are seen to be primordial, fundamental, reaching to the very heart of one's social being; seen of course not by the observer, but by the participants in ethnic interactions and conflicts.

We must start from an acceptance of the gap between the observer's view of reality and the subjective, and often irrational meanings, that people use to make sense of their worlds. 'What is real in the mind, is real in its consequences' is a tried and tested sociological adage. Let me illustrate this idea with a simple example at the individual level.

You hear a killer is loose, but you have no alternative but to walk along a dark alley to get home. 'Just in case', you have armed yourself with a kitchen knife. A silent stranger comes towards you and suddenly reaches into his pocket. You panic, thinking it's a gun and stab him. Then with horror you realise the man had a notebook in his hand, not a gun. He was mute and the notebook reads 'Help me, I'm lost'. You have killed an innocent man through a fatal misperception.

Now transpose this idea to a social setting. If, say, Croats believe that the Serbs are about to bomb their cities, loot their property, rape their women and murder their children, they will seek to defend themselves or will anticipate an attack by initiating one themselves. The Serbs respond in kind thus reinforcing the Croat's original perception that Serbs are bombers, looters, rapists and murderers. Fiercer attacks are therefore justified. Within a short time historical battles are recalled, vengeance is afoot and further recriminations and atrocities transpire.

The mechanisms involved in these encounters are certainly irrational, but they are not inexplicable. Fear of the unknown and heterophobia (the fear of difference) are both marked by a psychological state of unease, extreme anxiety, discomfort and a sense of loss of control.[8] Competition over jobs, desirable sexual partners, housing, status or territory compounds psychological *angst*, driving it into a higher gear. Sensing attack, you seek a bond with your friends and a clearer definition of your enemies. This bonding is sometimes so powerful that some people think it is sacred. The ethnic group, sometimes even the whole nation, becomes an object of worship, a civil religion for which you are prepared to die. The slogans 'White is right', 'For King and country', 'Deutschland über alles' and 'black power' seem paltry-enough ideas to an intellectual sophisticate, but they are real enough to the many people who believe in them.

CONCLUSION

I have suggested that my defence of the primordialist case is a limited, not an uncritical one. I do not accord any elevated epistemological status to primordial accounts – which are better regarded as descriptions not as explanations. Certainly, I could not, do not, accept any notion that ethnic differences are biologically programmed or divinely sanctioned. Put another way, ethnic consciousness is not transmitted through blood-lines nor is it supported by a sacred purpose. But the primordialists must undoubtedly be credited with demonstrating that ethnicity is a powerful and enduring social force, one that has been systematically underestimated by those – Marxists, nationalists and globalists – who wish it were not so.

Again, there are a number of extraneous processes – legal and political compulsion, migration and differential incorporation, the appearances of the different groups – that constrain and to a degree determine how ethnicity is manifested. These political, sociological and phenotypical constraints are rarely given full weight in the case made by social constructionists – who imply a higher degree of choice in the fabrication of an ethnic identity than is necessarily warranted. By contrast, my core argument is that it would be very foolish for any social scientist to ignore the fact that many individuals strongly believe that ethnic allegiances are part of their core identity and have to be defended on a life-or-death basis. In the process of people coming to these beliefs, one can argue that primordialism is itself being socially constructed.[9] Social identities differ not in that some are socially constructed while others are not. Rather, there is a marked incapacity to deconstruct primordial identities which, for the participants, take on the appearance of a God-given truth or a life-or-death struggle. They think they have far too much to lose to lightly cast away their ethnic garments.

Globalisation, political instability, the collapse of communism and the bloody fights for self-determination all over the globe have re-energised the primordial standard-bearers – ethnicity, tribe, race, language, religion and nation. Such conflicts and the sentiments that fuel them may – indeed do undoubtedly – have underlying causal elements. But these conflicts are defined, understood and accepted as primordial by their participants. And as many grieving families know, ethnic conflicts can become very real in their consequences.

NOTES ON CHAPTER 1

1 Robin Cohen is Professor of Sociology at the University of Warwick and a former director of its Centre for Research in Ethnic Relations. His recent books are *Frontiers of Identity: The British and the Others* (London: Longman 1994); *The Cambridge Survey of World Migration* (ed.) (Cambridge: Cambridge University Press, 1995); and *Global Diasporas: an Introduction* (London: UCL, 1997).
2 Cited in Nathan Glazer and Daniel P. Moynihan, *Beyond the Melting Pot: The Negros, Puerto Ricans, Jews, Italians and Irish of New York City* (Cambridge, MA: MIT Press, 1963), pp 289–90.
3 Typical is Jack David Eller and Reed M. Coughlin 'The poverty of primordialism: the demystification of ethnic sentiments', *Ethnic and Racial Studies* 16 (2), pp 183–202.
4 Edward Shils, 'Primordial, personal, sacred and civil ties', *British Journal of Sociology* 8 (2), pp 130–45; Clifford Geertz, 'The integrative revolution: primordial sentiments and civil politics in the new states (1963) in *The Interpretation of Culture: Selected Essays by Clifford Geertz* (New York: Basic Books, 1973), p 259.
5 Geertz, *The Interpretation of Culture*, p 259.
6 This passage paraphrases Anton Allahar 'More than an oxymoron: ethnicity and the social construction of primordial attachment', unpublished paper, Dept of Sociology, University of Western Ontario (London, Ontario, Canada, 1994). This insightful paper was subsequently published in the *Canadian Journal of Ethnic Studies* in 1995.
7 Stuart Hall 'The local and the global' in *Culture, Globalisation and the World System: Contemporary Conditions for the Representations of Identity*, ed. A.D. King (London: Macmillan, 1991).
8 Zigmund Bauman, *Modernity and the Holocaust* (Cambridge: Polity Press, 1991), pp 62–82, in elaborating Pierre André Taguieff, *La Force du préjugé: essai sur le racism et ses doubles* (Paris: La Decouverte 1988).
9 This is Allahar's main point in 'More than an oxymoron'.

2

THE NATURE OF ETHNICITY: LESSONS FROM AFRICA

Terence Ranger[1]

INTRODUCTION

Instead of finding myself in a life-and-death argument with some extreme primordialist, I find it impossible violently to disagree with the moderate Robin Cohen. But joking apart, his reasonable summary of the primordialist position compels me to start my rather differently to how I had intended. I had planned to go straight into my demonstration that ethnicity in much of Africa had been invented or imagined very recently, but it is now necessary first to respond to his account of prior, core, necessary identities.

In pre-colonial Africa, after all, there were certainly what Robin Cohen calls 'the givens' – 'congruities of blood, speech and culture', of 'common blood, kinship and belief'. If these amounted to ethnicity, how could I claim that it was recently invented? And if they were not the ingredients of ethnicity, what identities did they underlie? Cohen's challenge reinforces an older challenge from within Africa itself. In 1984, I gave a lecture in Zambia about the invention of tribalism.[2] As the audience filed out, I heard the Zambian Dean of Arts say to a colleague, 'Who were we then?' Once it has been imagined, ethnicity certainly seems primordial, and it becomes impossible to conceive of any prior identity. To claim that ethnicity did not exist in pre-colonial Africa seems like claiming that Africans had no identity at all. Of course, I would never want to assert anything so stupid or insulting, so I have increasingly realised the necessity for constructionist historians of ethnicity to offer an account of identities before it was constructed.

AFRICAN IDENTITIES BEFORE ETHNICITY

It has often been asserted that Africa is the ethnic continent *par excellence*. Textbooks on Africa have maps showing hundreds of 'tribes'. Even the splendid catalogue of the Royal Academy's current exhibition of African art, while noting that the word 'tribe' is no longer respectable, contains regional maps locating 'cultural groups' and 'peoples' whose names just happen to be exactly the same as the 'tribes' they have displaced.[3] And the Academy's exhibition covers thousands of years of African art. It seems that we cannot manage to think about Africa without invoking ethnicity.

Some people, indeed, claim that Africa is so useful to students of ethnicity because tribalism has persisted there from antiquity to the present, only imperfectly giving way to confessional, national or class identities. Hence, for them, African ethnicity is ethnicity in its primal state. I shall make exactly the opposite claim. Africa is invaluable to students of ethnicity precisely because that ethnicity is so recent there. We can study how it was made, and we can discover what there was before it.

It is necessary, first, to define what I mean by ethnicity. In Africa I equate it with 'tribalism', that is to say, the self conscious existence of a fairly large group of people who share the same language, operate with the same political, judicial and religious ideas, and hold the same myths of historical origin. Such located and bounded groups are held to constitute the primary sources of consciousness and identity. A simple, but implausible, way of maintaining that such an ethnicity is derived from the 'givens' of blood and kinship is to see a tribal society as consisting of thousands of 'natural' families, all descending from some original family.[4] Yet the idea of kinship, the idea of language and the idea of belief have no necessary connection with ethnicity at all.

Let me examine 'the givens' more closely, and begin with 'blood' (or I suppose we would say 'genes' nowadays) and 'kinship'. Genes certainly are given, but kinship – even what Robin Cohen calls 'parenthood' – is not. It was one of the truisms, and also one of the truths, of Africanist functionalist anthropology that kinship is itself constructed. There is no such thing as a 'natural' family. Everything about it, except that women give birth, is determined by historically produced social agreements which extend over areas far wider than any single ethnicity, but which can change and develop. Whether the wife lives with the husband's family or vice versa; whether the son 'belongs' to the father or to the maternal uncle; who inherits ranks and who inherits property; whether children grow up with their parents or away from them; whether brothers and sisters feel solidarity with each other or with their age-mates – all this and much more is socially and historically determined.

Family is not only constructed, but also acts as a metaphor. The titles 'father', 'mother', 'son', 'daughter' are not genetically given. They too are socially and historically determined. Young people of different 'blood', of different culture and even of different language can be and often have been integrated into African 'families'. Such families are units of identity and adherence, whether voluntary or coerced, and they often have little to do with ethnicity. No one identity is 'given' by the idea of kinship; many different identities can be constructed around it.

In particular, it is important to note that what we nowadays call a 'tribe' has a very complex relationship to kinship. 'Tribes' are much larger than the common-sense-perceived sum of kinship relations. The tribe can be imagined as a kin group only by exceptional intellectuals in very particular circumstances. The metaphor of kinship gives rise to other forms of identity much more easily. The African 'extended family' which we distinguish from our own 'nuclear families' is still a family rather than a tribe. When it enlarges it usually does so on the basis of what anthropologists call 'fictive' rather than biological kinship. It then becomes something like an early modern English aristocratic 'connection', but not something like an ethnicity.

The family as metaphor has often been used in Africa to bind together in defined relations of inequality people of many different origins. A recent striking statement of this can be found in a thorough study of Cape slavery by Robert Shell.[5] Shell asserts that in South African historiography 'frontier, class and settler-autochthonous relationships have been over-emphasised' – and he might have added 'ethnic relationships' to that list. 'A more fruitful way to explore the early years of the South African colonial past is to look at the domestic household. The family was the source of all concepts and patterns of subordination' and incorporation.

Shell insists that 'all members of the household, free and unfree, male and female, young and old, native, creole (locally born), mulatto (creole of mixed descent), and imported' were part of a single, though grossly inegalitarian, unit of identity. The family was an effective unit for incorporating slaves because 'blood' kin were themselves subject to authority – 'women and children in slave-owning families were on the same low level as the slaves and servants'. The family model was neither benevolent nor non-violent. Indeed, violence was intrinsic to family governance.

These Cape households were not held together by either blood or language. In a chapter entitled 'The Tower of Babel', Shell shows that every slave-holding household contained wide 'cultural and linguistic mixtures', and that 'Cape homesteads were nearly always inhabited by somatic and linguistic strangers'. He gives the example of Pieter van der Bijl's 'extended family', which included speakers of Dutch, French, Hindi, Khoi, Malay and Portuguese. Out of this extraordinary mixture there eventually arose the Creole language of Afrikaans, which was accompanied by what Shell calls 'biological creolisation'. Of course, when Afrikaaner intellectuals much later proclaimed an Afrikaaner ethnicity, they did their best to conceal these origins. In the twentieth century – the ethnic century par excellence – they succeeded in replacing the history of household and plantation creolisation with the history of a pre-destined *volk*.

Stimulating though this revisionist view of Cape history is, you may be objecting that Cape slave households were very atypical of African social formations. Yet, as Shell writes, 'anthropologists have fruitfully studied the complex kin networks and chain reactions to which the incorporation of slaves into households in other African societies gave rise'. Nineteenth century British missionaries in the Niger Delta recorded the dominance of the family metaphor, even if in terms rather more sentimental than Shell's. William Waddell found:

> Absolute authority on the one part and entire subjection on the other, is the theory; but in practice both the authority and the subjection are checked and limited in many ways... The harsh terms master and mistress are not in the Calabar language. The sweet and precious names, father and mother, alone are used to express the relation.[6]

Yet, of course, the 'fatherly' head of the Calabar 'House' presided over a family largely made up not of kin but of slaves from many different language groups. 'Familial' discipline was as ferocious as in the Cape and, as there, might extend to both slave and kin. But at the same time the fictive family of the 'House' served as a unit of identity. 'It is remarkable,' wrote Hugh Goldie, 'how clannish the slaves belonging to the same house become. Each one considers that he partakes of the honour of the house and is zealous in maintaining it. Any slight upon his... father is resented as a personal offence.' Plainly the Houses were institutions in their own right, and not expressions of Ibo – or even Kalibari – ethnicity.

Once again, you may object that this example too is a distortion found only on the slaving coast. Yet Joseph Miller has shown how 'families' were also reconstructed radically in the deep African interior. Elders followed the logic that 'goods obtainable [by selling] a young male could buy a slave wife capable, in time, of bearing children who would more than replace the youth lost'. So 'lords and elders aggregated young women and in effect bred children with whom they hoped to surround themselves in an honored old age'. In central Angola, Miller writes:

> visitors would have gotten the impression of villages filled with women and children, with the prepubertal girls out-numbering the boys. Men would be striking only by their absence. The number of young wives surrounding older males astonished visitors to the interior.[7]

Plainly, here too these reconstructed families were not bases for what Miller calls the 'stereotyped ethnic or "tribal" labels familiar in twentieth century Africa'.

Yet I shall allow one final objection. This, it can validly be said, is still an effect of the slaving system. Perhaps all these fictive family units of identity were part of an erosion of pre-existing ethnicity? Miller's reconstruction of Angolan societies before the rise of the slave trade gives little support to such a view. He discerns 'vague ancient communalities' experienced by groups originally coming from many different areas but sharing in the exploitation of a particular environment. Then in the eighteenth century these were overlaid, by 'better-defined political systems of lordship and tribute' which provided new primary political identities. Miller describes not a 'Lunda' tribe but a 'network of Lunda rulers – really a chain of political islands in a sea of woodlands occupied mostly by dispersed villagers recognising no overlord at all'. Even before slavery, several of these Lunda lords assembled 'locally powerful retinues for a lifetime or so'; and the household heads of the dispersed villages absorbed into their families 'pawns' or clients. Before slavery, then, there were household identities and aristocratic lineage identities; identities of place or of political connection, but not of tribe.[8]

Nor was language essential to these varying identities. Shell's Cape households were Towers of Babel; Dike's Houses incorporated speakers of many different languages; so did Miller's polygamous villages. In the end, these entities developed their own *lingua franca*, or the weaker aliens had to adopt the language of the master/father. But this is very different, of course, from communities brought up from birth in some ancestral 'mother-tongue'.

Moreover, co-existence of languages was even more characteristic of pre-colonial Africa than these forced incorporations into a common language. Miller's picture of Lunda lordlings occupying political islands in a sea of woodlands is also a picture of linguistic diversity. Even when a 'Lunda Empire' developed as a system of over-rule it did not involve linguistic homogeneity. Only under colonialism, when the Lunda became a major ethnic and tribal category, was it assumed that every Lunda spoke the same language.

Achim von Oppen has worked on 'Upper Zambezia', where under colonialism territorially-bounded ethnic and tribal classifications were carved out and tribal/linguistic names allocated to them. Prior to colonial rule, however, a constant feature of Upper Zambezi societies was 'a remarkable spatial mobility. Entire hamlets and individual members, both men and women, regularly used... to move to other sites several times in a lifetime.' They did so for

> a variety, often a combination, of economic and social factors, such as exhaustion of soil, water and game resources; trade; marriage; death; authority conflicts and other, often violent, tensions... A multitude of relationships, again often spanning enormous distances, were constantly constructed and negotiated between 'villages' and individuals. Both friendship and kinship idioms are used in the process, but they regularly include a strong element of negotiation and contract.[9]

As with Miller's eastern Angolan societies, people drew 'much of their identity from the particular kind of landscape' they shared and worked on.[10] Regional nicknames were applied to people in a particular environment. Four or five 'languages' developed out of a common central Bantu, but the major feature of the area was nevertheless linguistic interaction. As von Oppen notes, most students of the area have tried to reconcile their data with the 'colonial discourse' of ethnicity and territory, but

> Intra-regional, trans-ethnic linkages [still] represent an important aspect in the identity of the researched themselves. Among the inhabitants of this region, both the homogenous cultural background and high spatial mobility meant that members of different ethnic affiliations were in constant touch with each other. Today, initiation ceremonies, marriages, friendship, productive co-operation or joint business ventures very frequently cross [modern] ethnic boundaries; almost every child can communicate in at least two of the local languages.[11]

As he also notes, 'there are many indications that the same was true in the pre-colonial period... Here perhaps more than elsewhere ethnicity appears as an ideology of struggles for scarce resources and political realignment, like competition between rival brothers, rather than as an expression of real structural difference or distinction.' He cites Kubik's finding that there exists 'such a degree of ethnic, linguistic and cultural mixing' that it is more appropriate to speak of a 'regional culture' than of the 'cultures of individual ethnic groups'. Many of the most important defining relationships, whether ritual, religious or economic, not only facilitated but demanded multi-lingualism.

It is true, of course, that both Miller and von Oppen are dealing with a huge zone of peculiar fluidity and interaction. Nevertheless, in my own work on western Zimbabwe, where a series of over-rule 'states' were replaced in the nineteenth century by the much more authoritarian and structured Ndebele kingdom, most of their propositions remain true. 'Ndebele' ethnicity and the idea of an 'Ndebele' tribe speaking only Sindebele are a product of the last hundred years. In the nineteenth century western Zimbabwe was a zone of intense linguistic interaction. Sindebele was the language of the kingdom's rulers and of its regiments, but its members included speakers of Kalanga, Venda, Nyubi, Sotho and other tongues. When King Lobengula allocated the Jesuit missionaries Empandeni, the place of mixing, as the site of their huge farm, the missionaries found the young men speaking Sindebele and began to write about their tenants as typical Ndebele. They soon discovered that these young men were members of conquered groups being absorbed into the kingdom's regimental system; their wives spoke Kalanga; and the Empandeni missionaries eventually came to write studies of typical Kalanga culture. But this desire to elevate one identity over another, and to correlate it with language, was much more characteristic of missionary than of indigenous thought.[12]

Within the Ndebele kingdom lay the rain shrines of the High God, Mwali. Pilgrims came to them from all over the kingdom and from much further afield. Sindebele-speaking messengers came from the Kings with gifts of cattle; Banyubi, Kalanga, Karanga and Venda-speakers came with seeds to be blessed and with entreaties for rain. The priests at the shrine villages could handle all these languages and many more. 'God is language', they say today. Membership of the tributary and pilgrimage region of one of the Mwali shrines gave an identity. It defined people's relationships to the land; it linked people together along pilgrimage routes. In this way the people who lived within the Ndebele kingdom managed multiple identities: they were subjects of a powerful and prestigious polity; they were kinsmen in localised family groups; they were adepts of a regional cult. But they were not 'tribesmen'.[13]

As with everything else, scholarly treatments of African religion have been influenced by the colonial assumption of bounded identity. African religion has been regarded as microcosmic, dealing with face-to-face relations, and extending at most to a single 'tribe'. In fact, African religion expressed identities at every level from the household to the cult region. Like Christianity itself it was both macrocosmic and microcosmic in its implications.[14] Africans propitiated their own immediate ancestors, but they also joined hunting cults, went on pilgrimages to regional shrines, and were initiated into wide-ranging cults of spirit possession.

I think I have gone some way to demonstrating that 'blood' kinship, language and religion were not necessarily associated with ethnicity or tribal identity. I think too that I have given some answers to the Zambian Dean's question – 'Who were we before ethnicity?' African identities were given by and expressed in place, household, connection, occupation, polity, cult, and status – much like European identities in the medieval and early-modern period. As in Europe, there were also urban societies in Africa where identity was civic – like the Swahili-speaking cities of the East African coast.[15] Early modern Europeans who visited Africa were able to take these familiar identities seriously; later modern Europeans needed to find ethnicity.

MAKING ETHNICITY IN AFRICA

Robin Cohen remarked that scholars who insist on the constructedness of ethnicity tend to overplay subjective factors and to down-play objective ones. It is true that the words I have myself used to describe the process – 'invention' and 'imagination' – both imply intellectual processes rather than material ones.[16] But it is clear from what I have already said that both objective and subjective changes were necessary to produce and privilege ethnicity out of all the varying identities of pre-colonial Africa.

The analyses of Miller and von Oppen show that one thing that was needed to set the scene for territorially-bounded ethnicity was the disruption of the fluid and wide-ranging pre-colonial networks of trade, exchange, ritual participation etc. And colonialism involved just such a disruption. Trade and marketing was increasingly taken out of African hands; territorial and 'tribal' frontiers were established as barriers to the movement of villages and people. This happened everywhere, not only in Angola and Zambia. At one level the invention of tribes meant an enlargement of scale from the extended village; at another level it meant a great contraction of scale from the pre-colonial zones of interaction and exchange.

Von Oppen emphasises that ethnicity emerges as an ideology of competition for increasingly scarce resources, and this too was a feature of colonialism, whether the resources were land and water or access to education and employment. Competition for employment led to the phenomenon of urban ethnicity, in which groups of migrant workers contested for better-rewarded jobs on the basis of the arbitrary connections made between 'tribe' and occupation.[17] Robin Cohen also stressed competition between rival ethnicities, their differential incorporation into the colonial system and the emergence of 'ethnic-classes'.

Colonialism in Africa thus provided the objective requirements for the development of tribes as primary foci of identity. But I don't maintain that ethnicity could develop only under colonialism. It is possible for it to emerge wherever there are relations of inequality and exchange accompanied by intellectual assumptions of cultural and somatic classification. As John and Jean Comaroff write,

> In systems where 'ascribed' cultural differences rationalise structures of inequality, ethnicity takes on a cogent existential reality. It is this process of reification that gives it the appearance of being an autonomous factor in the ordering of the social world. As a result, ethnic identities regularly assume, for those who share them, a pervasive functionality in everyday social, economic and political life.[18]

In the Southern African case, Zulu ethnicity emerged in the early-nineteenth century in just such a context of inequality and differential incorporation into the Zulu state.[19] It has gone on being redefined and contested ever since. It is clear, though, that for Southern Africa, and for most of the rest of the continent, the late-nineteenth and early-twentieth centuries have been the key period for the emergence of tribalism. This has been partly due to the 'objective' factors already listed. But you will have noticed that 'subjective' factors have already crept in. The Comaroffs, speak of 'ascribed cultural differences'; the literature on early Zulu ethnicity speaks of ideology, as well as of power; I myself have suggested that 'intellectual assumptions of cultural and somatic classification' must accompany relations of inequality and exchange to produce the ideal breeding-ground for tribalism.

There is nothing dangerously abstract and intellectualist about these emphases. Bearing in mind what I have said above about the fluidity of language and religion in pre-colonial Africa, there obviously had to be decisive intellectual interventions to bring about a tribal homogeneity of 'people', territory, language and religion. Many of these interventions were made by missionaries. Patrick Harries has brilliantly described the process of missionary language invention as it took place in late nineteenth century Mozambique. He emphasises that the people of the coastal plain did not share a single language:

> In the south, west and north, the coastal language forms had been influenced, to a fluctuating degree, by the Zulu, Swazi and Gaza. Because of the political cleavages and the low degree of social and economic intercourse between the chiefdoms, the peoples east of the Lebombos had never needed a common, unifying language. Indeed, the different chiefdoms stressed their independence of one another by magnifying their differences of language and accent... The Swiss missionaries were struck by the enormity of their prospective mission field and by its prodigious linguistic diversity.

Such linguistic and ethnic disorder ran contrary to every instinct of the Swiss. They insisted that prior to recent invasions and disruptions there must have existed uniformity of identity and speech.

> The missionaries believed that... a large number of people shared the same linguistic past and that this (proto) Thonga language was rooted in prehistory. This belief in the primordialness of language dovetailed with the view, dominant in Europe at the time, that language was the major determinant of modes and patterns of thought. It was believed that people who spoke a common language possessed a similar code through which they interpreted the world. This equipped them with an ethos (almost a soul) that, consciously or unconsciously, bound them as a tribe or nation.[20]

So the missionaries 'revived' Thonga, turning it into a written language, using it in their churches and schools, and in effect creating a Thonga ethnicity.

Selecting out and privileging one language or dialect – and assuming that language was the prime marker of identity – took place throughout missionary Africa. Everywhere too there were interventions in the field of religion, both by the state and by the missionaries. As we have seen, in Angola or Upper Zambezia or south-western Zimbabwe – or, indeed, in the Mozambique coastal plain – there were wide networks of religious interaction and observance. The new colonial states did not like these networks. They feared that they might act as a means of inter-tribal co-operation or as a means of sending out orders to rebel – most anti-colonial resistance being explained as the result of 'superstition'. Everywhere colonial administrations tried to break up such networks and to harass their emissaries. Instead they valued and supported 'tribal' religion, and in particular the rituals which lent support to chiefs. Meanwhile, the missionaries, while preaching membership of the universal body of Christ, in effect created very localised churches, based in the village or at most in an ethnic *volk*. Thus the Afro-American scholar, Karen Fields, has argued that the ideology of 'indirect rule' in colonial Northern Rhodesia, with its systematic creation of 'tribes', was based both on chiefly cults and on mission Christianity.[21]

LIVING ETHNICITY IN AFRICA

Robin Cohen, allowing that many ethnicities were constructed, goes on to point out that this had little effect on their 'reality'. 'What is real in the mind,' he insists, 'is real in its consequences'. And of course this is true.

From the very beginning of the creation of tribalism in Africa the necessary intellectual processes were taking place in African as well as in European minds. Not even the most brilliant or forceful missionary could create a written language by himself. He depended on African informants and fellow translators, and it was in fact these teachers and evangelists who made the most effective use of the new written languages when they emerged. Among other things, they wrote 'tribal histories' of the new language groups, thereby giving ideological charters for the idea of their primordiality. They described local 'traditional religion'. They led the local churches. They were organic intellectuals for the *volk*. These men were no longer part of the pre-colonial networks of hunting and trade and resettlement. They operated out of the fixed points of mission schools, churches and clinics; the Christian cemetery was their locus of spiritual power; their identities were both confessional and ethnic.[22]

But these African Christian collaborators were for a long time a small minority. Most Africans did not become 'ethnic' or 'tribal' overnight. The wider networks could not be dismantled just like that. Colonial frontiers were permeable. Pilgrims still continued to visit the shrines of the High God in the Matopos mountains, even though in colonial Southern Rhodesia it was a criminal offence to leave one's tribal area without a pass from the Native Commissioner. Still, as literacy spread and residence was 'stabilised'; as migration took the form of men going off to the towns and mines rather than whole families and villages moving; as competition for colonial resources intensified, so more and more people came to identify themselves in ethnic and tribal terms. The overwhelming majority of women were now tied to their rural 'home'; in the towns, men came to organise themselves into ethnic associations. Ethnicity came to be more and more 'real in the mind'.

As it did so, it came more and more under African intellectual control and less and less defined by white administrators or missionaries. Whites could insist upon the primacy of certain languages, offer ethnic labels or subsidise 'tribal' chiefs. But they could not fill ethnicity with real imaginative and moral content. This was something that Africans did for themselves.

John Lonsdale has famously distinguished between 'political tribalism' – the manipulation of ethnicity by the state – and 'moral ethnicity' – the debate about class, gender and generation within a tribal group. As Cohen pointed out, the colonial or post-colonial state was too large (and it might be added, too amoral) to be an arena for determining the crucial issues of social change. Identities came not simply to be expressed ethnically but, more importantly, to be disputed within an ethnicity. Lonsdale has brilliantly analysed this dispute among 'the Kikuyu'; I have tried to follow his example for 'the Ndebele'. Many scholars are now doing the same for 'the Zulu'.[23]

THE FUTURE OF ETHNICITY IN AFRICA – AND ELSEWHERE

In many parts of Africa, ethnicity has well and truly become 'real in the mind' and 'real in its consequences'. There are all too many examples of political tribalism, as well as the continued working out of 'moral ethnicity'. The notion of ethnic primordiality has obstructed reconstruction of the African past as well as threatening class and national solidarities, and sometimes threatening civil war.[24] When I wrote *The Invention of Tribalism in Zimbabwe*, I assumed that it was desirable for ethnicity to be replaced by nationalism. The last words of that pamphlet are:

> It is important to show that tribal identity is not inevitable, unchanging, given, but a product of human creativity which can be re-invented and re-defined to become once again open, constructive and flexible, subordinate to other loyalties and associations which relate more directly to suffering and its relief.[25]

Nevertheless, I have come to realise that, just like nationalism, ethnicity is neither bad nor good in itself.[26] Everything depends on what views prevail in the moral debate within ethnicity. So I ended the section on ethnicity in my recent revisitation of tradition rather differently:

> In my 1985 pamphlet I was concerned to show the artificial and narrowly-based 'invention' of Ndebele tribalism and to emphasise that if people had come to think of themselves as primarily Ndebele they could as readily come to think of themselves as Zimbabweans. I think now that this was correct insofar as it emphasised historicity and self-consciousness, but misleading insofar as it opposed Ndebele and national identity. The issue in the Zimbabwean case – as with the Kikuyu in Kenya and the Zulu in South Africa – seems to be not how to move from reactionary tribalism to progressive

> nationalism, but how to ensure interactions between a dynamic and inclusive ethnicity and a democratic nationalism.[27]

This seems to me to be the case everywhere in Africa, and it needs as much work on making nationalism democratic as it does on imagining ethnicity as dynamic and inclusive. I think – to return at last to the general question of ethnicity and move away from the African example – that it is probably also the case in what used to be Yugoslavia and the Soviet Union, where the processes of classifying, inventing and imagining ethnic identities has been so much the same as in Africa.

At a St Antony's College Seminar on 'Tribe, State and Nation' in 1993, I gave a talk entitled 'Tribalisation of Africa: Retribalisation of Europe'.[28] I suggested that the word 'ethnicity' be banned from press reports on the Caucasus or Bosnia, but that scholars be urged to 'ask Lonsdale's moral ethnicity questions about Georgian, Serbian and Bosnian "identities"'. I ended by invoking recent literature on ethnicities in Britain itself:

> Even if political tribalism can be exposed and moral ethnicity understood, I do not know whether, in Africa or in Eastern Europe, people can take up Stuart Hall's call for everyone to imagine ethnic identities – rich, hybrid, mongrel, inclusive, ludic identities, operating within the confines of the nation-state as broker. And of course it would be especially good for me to think as an Africanist that our studies of tribalism and ethnicity in Africa might contribute towards these desirable outcomes.

This seems a good place at which to end an Africanist contribution to the study of the nature of ethnicity.

NOTES ON CHAPTER 2

1 Terence Ranger is recently retired as Rhodes Professor of Race Relations at the University of Oxford. He is author of many works, including *The Invention of Tribalism in Zimbabwe* (Gweru: Mambo, 1985); *The Invention of Tradition* (ed. with Eric Hobsbawm) (Cambridge: Cambridge University Press, 1992); *Legitimacy and the State in Twentieth-Century Africa* (ed, with Olufemi Vaughan) (London: St Antony's/ Macmillan, 1993). This paper is based on his contribution to the debate on ethnicity and nationalism held at Warwick University in 1995. Another version of this argument is to be found in Paris Yeros (ed.), *Ethnicity and Nationalism* (London: Macmillan, 1999).

2 This lecture was published in expanded form as *The Invention of Tribalism in Zimbabwe*.

3 Tom Phillips (ed.), *Africa: The Art of a Continent* (London: Royal Academy, 1995).

4 An example of this way of thinking is Aeneas Chigwedere's *Birth of Bantu Africa* (Bulawayo: Books for Africa, 1982), p 28. Chigwedere

writes that 'there were three Bantu families in all eastern Africa from the Great East African Lakes to at least the Limpopo around the year 900 AD... All Bantu Africa is populated by no more than segments of these three Great Bantu Families'. The three 'descended from a common ancestor' who 'had three wives' and from them descended the three great 'tribes' which populated the whole of Bantu Africa. All existing 'sub-tribes' are fragments of them. Chigwedere writes: 'The mother and father are the starting point of the tribe. The family grows until it constitutes a sub-tribe. The sub-tribe grows until it constitutes a tribe. The tribe then splits up into three or four segments. These segments in turn grow up into tribes and also split up. This is common knowledge to us, for new sub-tribes and tribes were forming all over Africa when we were overtaken by the events associated with the New Imperialism of the late nineteenth century. Indeed, has the formation of sub-tribes and tribes come to an end even today? What were mere individual families in 1890 in Zimbabwe have today grown into sub-tribes.'

5 Robert Shell, *Children of Bondage* (Johannesburg: University of the Witwatersrand, 1994).

6 Waddell and Goldie are quoted in K. Onwuka Dike's classic *Trade and Politics in the Niger Delta, 1830–1885* (Oxford: Clarendon Press, 1956), p 36.

7 Joseph Miller, *Way of Death* (Madison, University of Wisconsin, 1988), pp. 99, 163, 167.

8 The Nigerian scholar, Peter Ekeh, has argued that the slave trade, so far from undermining ethnicity, contributed to its emergence in the long term. During the time of slaving, people sought refuge in 'corporate kinship groups' from the oppression of the state. Under colonialism, these kinships groups were conceptually expanded 'into the construction of ethnic groups': Peter Ekeh, 'Social Anthropology and Two Contrasting Uses of Tribalism in Africa', *Comparative Studies in Society and History*, 32/4, October 1990.

9 Achim von Oppen, 'Mobile Practice and Local Identity', in Joachim Heidrich (ed.), *Changing Identities: The Transformation of Asian and African Societies under Colonialism* (Berlin: Centre for Modern Oriental Studies, 1994), pp 198–9.

10 Environmental identities could become sharply defined. In what is now Kenya, for example, 'Kikuyu' identity originally developed as the self-description of the many heterogeneous groups who combined to clear the forest for cultivation, while Maasai identity described a pastoralist commitment. Robin Cohen chose the Maasai to illustrate the limitations of ethnic choice, saying that if someone was Maasai he could not change to another ethnicity. In fact people could and did change from the Kikuyu to the Maasai identities, and vice versa, as they moved from one economic activity to another. Bruce Berman and John Lonsdale, *Unhappy Valley, Book Two: Violence and Ethnicity* (London: James Currey, 1992); Thomas Spear and Richard Waller (eds), *Being Maasai* (London: James Currey, 1993).

11 Achim von Oppen, *Terms of Trade and Terms of Trust* (Hamburg-Munster, 1994), pp 32–3.

12 I have developed my ideas about identity in Matabeleland in a series of chapters and articles of which the most recent are: 'The Invention of Tradition Revisited', in Terence Ranger and Olufemi Vaughan (eds), *Legitimacy and the State in Twentieth-Century Africa* (London: St Antony's/Macmillan, 1993); 'African Identities: Ethnicity, Nationality and History: The Case of Matabeleland, 1893–1993', in Joachim Heidrich (ed.), *Changing Identities* (Berlin: Center for Modern Oriental Studies, 1994). These discussions are based on research in central and southern Matabeleland. Recent research in northern Matabeleland, where the language, religious and 'ethnic' situation has been even more complicated, is deployed in 'The Moral Economy of Ethnicity in Northern Matabeleland', published in an Edinburgh African Studies Centre collection in 1996. The extreme 'ethnic' and linguistic fluidity of north-western Zimbabwe is described in Eric Worby, 'Maps, Names and Ethnic Games', *Journal of Southern African Studies*, 20/3, September 1994.

13 For the Mwali shrines, see R.P. Werbner (ed.), *Regional Cults* (London: Academic Press, 1977); J.M. Schoffeleers (ed.), *Guardians of the Land* (Gweru: Mambo, 1978); R.P. Werbner, *Ritual Passage: Sacred Journey* (Washington, Smithsonian, 1989). The history of the shrines in the context of the Matopos mountains is provided in Terence Ranger, *Voices From the Rocks* (London: James Currey, forthcoming).

14 Terence Ranger, 'The Local and the Global in Southern African Religious History' in Robert W. Hefner (ed.), *Conversion to Christianity* (Berkeley: UCP, 1993).

15 These East African cities are strikingly like medieval and early modern European towns in their expressions of identity and faction. I have heard it said, for instance, that carnival – with its mobilisation of quarters and factions – is peculiar to Catholic Europe. But competitive festive identity was expressed just as strongly on the East African coast: Terence Ranger, *Dance and Society in Eastern Africa* (London, HEB, 1975).

16 Terence Ranger, 'The Invention of Tradition in Colonial Africa' in Eric Hobsbawm and Terence Ranger (eds), *The Invention of Tradition* (Cambridge: CUP, 1983); 'The Invention of Tradition Revisited' in Terence Ranger and Olufemi Vaughan (eds), *Legitimacy and the State in Twentieth Century Africa* (London: St Antony/Macmillan, 1993).

17 Terence Ranger, 'Race and Tribe in Southern Africa: European Ideas and African Acceptance' in Robert Ross (ed.), *Racism and Colonialism* (Leiden, 1982).

18 John and Jean Comaroff, 'Of Totemism and Ethnicity' in *Ethnography and the Historical Imagination* (Boulder, Westview Press, 1992), p 61.

19 Catherine Hamilton, 'Ideology, Oral Traditions and the Struggle for Power in the Early Zulu Kingdom', MA thesis, University of the

Witwatersrand, 1986; John Wright, 'The Dynamics of Power and Conflict in the Thukela-Mzimkhulu Region in the Late Eighteenth and Early Nineteenth Centuries', PhD thesis, Wits, 1990; Catherine Hamilton and John Wright, 'The Making of the Amalala: Ethnicity, Ideology and Relations of Subordination in a Precolonial Context', *South African Historical Journal* 22, November 1990.

20 Patrick Harries, 'The Roots of Ethnicity: Discourse and the Politics of Language Construction in South-East Africa', *African Affairs* 87/436, January 1988, pp 34, 39. I have treated another case of missionary creation of ethnicity through language in my 'Missionaries, Migrants and the Manyika: The Invention of Ethnicity in Zimbabwe' in Leroy Vail (ed.), *The Creation of Tribalism in Southern Africa* (London, James Currey, 1989). Ironically in this case missionary language work fragmented a genuine very large zone of a single 'Shona' language into regional dialectical ethnicities.

21 Karen Fields, *Revival and Rebellion in Colonial Central Africa* (Princeton: Princeton University Press, 1985). I have discussed the localising and ethnicising effect of the colonial state in Terence Ranger, 'Religious Movements and Politics in Sub-Saharan Africa', *African Studies Review* 29/2, June 1986, and in 'The Local and the Global in Southern African Religious History' in R.W. Hefner (ed.), *Conversion to Christianity* (UCP, 1993).

22 I have described these ideological initiatives of African Christians in 'Protestant Missions in Africa: The Dialectic of Conversion' in T.D. Blakely, W.E.A. van Beek and D.L. Thomson (eds), *Religion in Africa* (London: James Currey, 1994).

23 John Lonsdale, 'The Moral Economy of Mau-Mau' in Bruce Berman and John Lonsdale, *Unhappy Valley* (London: James Currey, 1992); Terence Ranger, 'The Invention of Tradition Revisited'; Gerhard Mare, *Ethnicity and Politics in South Africa* (London: Zed, 1993); Patrick Harries, 'Imagery, Symbolism and Tradition in a South African Bantustan' in V.Y. Mudimbe and B. Jewsiewicki (eds), *History Making in Africa: History and Theory* 32, 1993.

24 Two recent treatments of ethnicity in contemporary African politics are K.E. Friedman and A. Sundberg, 'Ethnic War and Ethnic Cleansing in Brazzaville' and Mahmood Mamdani, 'Indirect Rule, Civil Society and Ethnicity' in Preben Kaarsholm (ed.), *From Post-Traditional to Post Modern?* (Roskilde: IDS, 1995).

25 The Invention of Tribalism in Zimbabwe, *op. cit.*, p. 19.

26 Mamdani writes that 'ethnicity was never just about identity. Its two contradictory moments involved both social control and social emancipation. This is why it makes sense neither just to embrace ethnicity uncritically nor simply to reject it one-sidedly.' 'Indirect Rule', *op. cit.*, p. 223.

27 'The Invention of Tradition Revisited', *op. cit.*, pp. 100–1.

28 This was printed in *The Woodstock Road Editorial: An Oxford Magazine of International Affairs* 16, Hilary, 1994.

PART II

NATION

3

ADAM'S NAVEL: 'PRIMORDIALISTS' VERSUS 'MODERNISTS'

Ernest Gellner[1]

FOREWORD

Ernest Gellner died on 5 November 1995 in Prague, the city where he lived as a child and to which he returned in 1992 to establish the Centre for the Study of Nationalism. In September this year the centre accepted its first group of doctoral students, one of whom remembered their teacher in the following words.

> We never dared to address Professor Gellner by his first name. 'Call me Ernest, please,' he insisted, but we remained too awe-struck. His first response to our papers was always, 'Such and such was interesting, but...' Professor Gellner was famous for his 'but'. To us graduate students from all over Central and Eastern Europe, just starting our academic careers, he was tolerance and inspiration itself. He never seemed bored by our ideas or petty problems, and never missed a chance to make us feel important. At the last conference we attended with him, he told us to speak up because he wanted to hear, loud and clear, our names and the title of his brainchild – The Centre for the Study of Nationalism, Central European University, Prague. He was not a frivolous man and could be a demanding teacher, but he smiled upon us and made us laugh. At receptions, he would always make sure that our glasses were full.

> And we fidgeted with nervous excitement whenever we bumped into him in the student residence in Prokopova Street. He lived there with us and never complained about our parties or having to queue with us for the telephone. Outside on the streets of Prague we could spot him by the raffish hats he wore. Professor Gellner taught us the excitement of learning and the principles of academic debate. We shall not forget that – or him.'[2]

* * *

It is a source of great pride to me that my student, Anthony Smith, should become one of the leading specialists on nationalism. We have long been in debate with one another, and it is useful in debate to draw up clear battle lines. He and I tend to be pitted against each other on opposite sides of what has become the major dividing line in the study of nationalism – the line between what I call 'primordialists' and 'modernists'. The primordialists say that nations were there all the time (or some of them were, anyway) and that the past matters a great deal. The modernists such as myself believe that the world was created at about the end of the eighteenth century, and that nothing which happened before makes the slightest difference to the issues we face.

The question is: how do you decide between the two? What kind of evidence can we use to establish the reality of the past? Bertrand Russell once asked, tongue in cheek, how do we know that the world was not created five minutes ago, complete with memories? Well, how do you know? Maybe it was. What is the evidence? Another form this debate takes is the battle between creationists and evolutionists. Was mankind created with Adam or did it slowly evolve? At the time when the evidence was debated, a particular question was very much alive: did Adam have or did he not have a navel? This is a crucial question. You may fall about laughing, but obviously if Adam was created by God at a certain date, 4003BC say, it is a natural first reaction to say that he did not have a navel, because Adam did not go through the process by which people acquire navels. It is very simple. We actually know what question will decide whether the world is very old and mankind evolved, or whether the world was created about 6000 years ago. All we need to find out is whether or not Adam had a navel.

The question I am now about to address is: do nations have navels or do they not? The case for modernism is that the ethnic, the cultural and the national community is rather like the navel. Some nations have one, some don't. Either way it is not essential.

What Anthony is saying, on the other hand, is that he is anti-creationist. He believes that we have this plethora of navels and that they are absolutely essential. He says – and I think this is the crux of the disagreement between us – that modernism only tells half the story. But if it tells half the story, that is enough for me.

There are some very clear cases where modernism holds true. Take the Estonians. At the beginning of the nineteenth century they did not even have a name for themselves. They were simply referred to as people who lived on the land, as opposed to German or Swedish burghers and aristocrats and Russian administrators. They were just a category without any ethnic self-consciousness. But since then, they have been brilliantly successful in creating a vibrant culture which can be seen, very much alive, in the ethnographic museum in Tartu. The museum has one object for every Estonian – and there are one million Estonians. Obviously, Estonian culture is under no threat, although Estonians make a fuss about the Russian minority which they have inherited from the Soviet system. Estonians have a vital and vibrant culture, but it was created by the kind of modernist process which I apply to nationalism and nations in general. If that kind of account holds true for some nations, then the exceptions which are credited to other nations are redundant.

The central fact of the modern world is that the role of culture in human life was totally transformed by the cluster of economic and scientific changes since the seventeenth century. The prime role of culture in agrarian society was to underwrite a people's status and identity – to entrench their position in a complex, usually hierarchical, relatively stable structure. In today's world people have no stable position within a structure. They are members of ephemeral professional bureaucracies which are not deeply internalised. They belong to increasingly loose family associations. And what really matters is how they can incorporate and master high culture. By that I mean a literate codified culture which permits context-free communication, community membership and acceptability – that is what constitutes a nation. It is a consequence of the mobility and anonymity of modern society, and of the semantic, non-physical nature of our work, that makes mastery of such culture, and acceptance within it, the most valuable possessions an individual has. It is a pre-condition of all other privileges and participation in society. This is what automatically makes people into nationalists, because if there is no congruence between the culture in which they are operating and the culture of the surrounding economic, political and educational bureaucracies, then they are in trouble. They and their offspring will be exposed to sustained humiliation.

Moreover, the maintenance of the high culture, the medium in which society operates, is politically precarious and expensive. The state is the protector, usually the financier – or at very least the quality controller – of the educational process which shapes people into members of this high culture. This is a process of creation – my equivalent of that event of 6000BC when humanity was suddenly brought into being.

Anthony Smith makes a number of points with which I would in no way disagree. Culture, or at least a shared form of symbols and communication, was important even in the pre-industrial age. That is indisputable – so having a 'one-navel' culture was then a central feature of societies. Culture carries a great emotional charge, and its members are highly conscious of their participation in it. The ancient Greeks knew the difference between people who read Homer and those who did not. Ancient Greeks knew the difference between people who were allowed to participate in the Olympic games and those who were not. They had a deep contempt for barbarians, who fell into the inferior class. In that sense they were plainly cultural chauvinists.

So cultures are sometimes conscious and beloved, and sometimes invisible and ignored. Sometimes, too – but this is less likely – they have political institutions connected to them. But, generally speaking, the condition of the agrarian world favoured political units consisting of local, intimate communities which were smaller than a 'culture', or much larger units such as large empires. There was nothing in the logic of the political situation to lead political units to expand to the boundaries of the culture. They tended to be either smaller or larger. Sometimes a culture expressed itself politically, but more often it did not. Sometimes there was continuity between the cultures which were loved in the pre-industrial age and sometimes there was discontinuity.

As an example, I would not say that there is either a genuine folk memory or a preoccupation with Periclean Athens in modern Greece. There is some continuity with Byzantium, or at any rate with the clerical organisation which it left behind. Therefore, I would say that there is a certain amount of navel about, but not in every example, and on the whole it is not vital – it is not like the cycles of respiration, blood circulation or food digestion which Adam would have had to have in order to live at the moment of creation. You would have to have a kind of fictitious past and yet that past, would also have to be real. This is why I believe that cultural continuity is contingent and inessential.

Where does this leave us? I think the evolutionists are slightly unfair in saying that I am only interested in how nations came about, and not in how they behave. Obviously it does matter to predict which nations will assert themselves and, in the case of potential nations, which cultural categories will assert themselves and which will not. But it is inherent to the situation that you cannot make exact predictions – you can only point to certain factors. Size is an obvious one, as very small cultural groups tend to give up. Continuity is another factor, but not an essential one; some diaspora communities have asserted themselves very effectively. Size, continuity, and the existence of symbolism are important – but again, the Estonians created nationalism out of thin air in the course of the nineteenth century.

The agrarian world was enormously rich in cultural nuance; the modern world has space for only two or three hundred national states. Not all potential nations become real ones, and many do not even try. I do not believe you can apply any simple formula for identifying which ones will become real. So we can conclude that the modernists have a greater sense of how nations invent their navels, as opposed to how they inherit them.

NOTES ON CHAPTER 3

1 The late Ernest Gellner was Professor, and founder, of the Centre for the Study of Nationalism at the Central European University in Prague until his death in November 1995, some 11 days after his participation in the Warwick Debates on 24 October 1995. This paper was the written version of his contribution to the debate with Prof. Anthony Smith. Ernest Gellner was the author of many distinguished works, including: *Nations and Nationalism* (Oxford: Basil Blackwell, 1990); *Reason and Culture* (Oxford: Blackwell, 1992); *Encounters with Nationalism* (Oxford: Blackwell, 1994); *Conditions of Liberty* (London: Hamish Hamilton, 1994).

2 Re-printed from *Prospect*, December 1995.

4

THE NATION: REAL OR IMAGINED?

Anthony D. Smith[1]

I greatly appreciate the achievement and the inspiration provided to me, and to all of us, by Ernest Gellner. It was his work that first caught my imagination in 1964, when I was groping for a method of studying phenomena that had already for some time absorbed me and that were, after the wave of decolonisation in Africa and Asia, very much in the air. Not only did Gellner encourage and guide my thesis on theories of nationalism with such patience and care; he taught me three fundamental lessons about nations and nationalism which have served as a guide thereafter.

The first lesson is that nationalism is elusive, even protean, in its manifestations, and that we have to try to classify the rich variety of movements and ideologies which go under the name of nationalism if we are to make any progress in understanding so variegated a phenomenon.

Second, he taught me to appreciate the underlying sociological reality of nationalism and its creation, the nation. Against all those who would tell us that the nation exists only in the imagination and that it can be deconstructed away, Gellner has always insisted that nations and nationalism are real and powerful sociological phenomena, even if their reality is quite different from the tale told about them by nationalists themselves.

Third, he convinced me that nations, as well as nationalisms, are modern phenomena, in the sense that the basic features of the modern world require nations and nationalisms. You could not have one without the other. This is obvious in the case of nationalism, the ideological movement, which clearly did not exist before the eighteenth century. But it is also true of nations in general. That is to say, even if a few nations were to be found before the advent of modernity, most nations are relatively recent, and are necessarily modern.

And yet there is at this point a certain difference between Gellner and myself. Insofar as he is a wholehearted 'modernist', Gellner would claim that the nation is not only relatively recent; it is also the product of specifically modern conditions – those of early industrialism or its anticipations, social mobility, the need for mass literacy, public education and the like. It is the modern transition from spontaneous, non-literate 'low' cultures to highly cultivated, literate and specialised 'high' cultures that engenders nationalism and nations.[2] It is not that I find this account wrong, but that it only tells half the story. There is another half, and other ways of looking at this protean phenomenon. I shall try to tell this other half and consider some of these other ways.

I think most of us would agree that nationalism is today one of the most powerful forces in the world, and that the national state has been for a century at least, and continues to be, the cornerstone of international politics. Nationalism provides the sole legitimation of states the world over, including the many polyethnic and federal ones. It is also the most widespread and popular ideology and movement, and it comes as no surprise that many of the world's most intractable conflicts – in India and the Middle East, the Caucasus and the Horn of Africa, the Balkans and southern Africa – are either ethno-national conflicts or possess a strong nationalist component.

Of course it is easy to exaggerate the influence of nationalism, and to inflate the terms nation and nationalism, to cover every aspect of a state's social, cultural and political policy, and every dimension of inter-state relations. The first thing, therefore, is to define our concepts.

By 'nationalism' I mean an ideological movement for the attainment and maintenance of autonomy, unity and identity of a human population, some of whose members conceive it to constitute an actual or potential 'nation'. By a 'nation' I mean a named human population sharing an historic territory, common myths and memories, a mass, public culture, a single economy and common rights and duties for all members. This definition suggests that the concept of the nation refers to a particular kind of social and cultural community, a territorial community of shared history and culture. This is the assumption of nationalists themselves, for whom the world is composed of unique historic culture-communities, to which its citizens owe a primary loyalty and which is the sole source of political power and inner freedom.[3]

It is important to distinguish the concept of the nation from that of the state. The state is a legal and political concept; states can be defined as autonomous, public institutions of coercion and extraction within a recognised territory. States are not communities.[4] We should also recall that the systems of states that arose, first in Europe and then in other parts of the world, often preceded the rise of nationalism, as well as many of today's nations, though not necessarily many of their core ethnic groups. This lack of temporal and spatial fit between state and nation is one of the main causes of many of today's national conflicts.[5]

For most people, nations, especially their own nations, appear to be perennial and immemorial. They cannot easily imagine a world without nations, nor are they happy with the idea that their nation is a recent creation or even a construct of elites. Indeed, an older generation of scholars, often under the unconscious influence of nationalism, tended to seek and find 'nations' everywhere, in all ages and continents.[6] Today, however, most scholars would regard the idea of nations existing perennially through antiquity and the middle ages as simply 'retrospective nationalism'. For most post-war scholars, nations and nationalisms are fairly recent phenomena, arising immediately before, during or in the wake of the French Revolution. They also tend to see nations and nationalisms as products of modernisation and features of modernity. Many of these 'modernist' theories are, at root, materialist. In some cases, the materialism is explicit. Tom Nairn, for example, regards nationalism as the product of, and response to, the 'uneven development' of capitalism.[7] In other cases, materialism is conceived as part and parcel of cultural processes of modernisation – be it the mobile society based on a public system of mass, standardised literary education which Ernest Gellner regards as critical, or the rise of reading publics engendered by the spread of the technology of 'print-capitalism' stressed by Benedict Anderson.[8] In all these cases, nations and nationalisms are viewed as more or less inevitable outgrowths of a modern, industrial society, however regrettable their consequences may be.[9]

It is, of course, in the 'deconstructive' models of Benedict Anderson and Eric Hobsbawm that the question of the real or imagined status of the nation has been most sharply posed. In

Hobsbawm's approach, the nation is seen, in large part, as a set of 'invented traditions' comprising national symbols, mythology and suitably tailored history.[10] In Anderson's model, the nation is seen as an 'imagined political community', one that is imagined as both finite and sovereign.[11] I do not think that either would regard the nation as a wholly imaginary construct; at the same time, they wish to debunk nationalist views of the nation as somehow 'primordial' and 'perennial'.[12]

This seems to me quite proper provided that, in designating the nation as an 'imagined community' or 'invented tradition', we do not gainsay its reality or consider it a fabrication. There is nothing contradictory about saying that something is both imagined and real: the Parthenon, Chartres and the Sistine ceiling are no less real and tangible for all the imagination of their creators and spectators down the ages. But if nations are not fabricated, are they cultural artefacts created in the same way as artistic monuments? I shall argue that, although we can often discern elements of deliberate planning and human creativity in their formation, nations and nationalisms are also the products of pre-existing traditions and heritages which have coalesced over the generations.

Let me return to the far more acceptable 'modernist' theories that emphasise the sociological reality of nations, once they have been formed. There are certain problems associated with these theories. The first is their generality. Though they make out a convincing case for explaining 'nationalism in general', they are often pitched at such a level of abstraction that they cannot be easily applied to specific areas or cases. They appear to cover everything, and yet when we look to them to illuminate actual historical instances, they so often invoke exceptional circumstances – like the religious factor, or colour, or a history of ethnic antagonism.[13]

Second, their materialism is often quite misleading. Nationalism can emerge in all kinds of socio-economic milieux – in rich Quebec and poor Eritrea, in areas of decline as well as improvement, in pre-industrial as well as industrial conditions. Nor is it easy to explain the content and intensity of particular nationalisms through the workings of global capitalism or the dynamics of relative deprivation.[14]

But the third problem is the most crucial, since it stems from the commitment to modernism as such: it is the idea that nations and nationalisms are the product of modernisation. What this systematically overlooks is the persistence of ethnic ties and cultural sentiments in many parts of the world and their continuing significance for large numbers of people. Eric Hobsbawm, indeed, goes so far as to deny any connection between the popular 'proto-national' communities that he analyses and subsequent political nationalisms.[15]

This is exactly where I disagree. Modern political nationalisms cannot be understood without reference to these earlier ethnic ties and memories, and in some cases to pre-modern ethnic identities and communities. I do not wish to assert that every modern nation must be founded on some antecedent ethnic ties, let alone a definite ethnic community; but many such nations have been and are based on these ties, including the first nations in the West – France, England, Castille, Holland, Sweden, and they acted as models and pioneers of the idea of the 'nation' for others. When we dig deeper, we find an ethnic component in many later national communities, whether the nation was formed slowly or was the outcome of a more concerted project of 'nation-building'.[16]

I believe that this kind of approach, which we may term 'ethno-symbolic', is more helpful for understanding the growth of nations, the rise of ethno-nationalisms and the conflicts to which they give rise. To begin with, it is an approach or perspective, not a theory. I doubt whether we are in a position yet to offer a theory of so protean and many-sided a set of phenomena as ethnies, nations and nationalisms, except at a very general level. Second, this kind of approach may help to explain which populations are likely to give rise to a nationalist movement under certain conditions, and what the content of their nationalism is likely to be – though there is much work to be done here. An exploration of earlier ethnic configurations will, I suggest, help us to explain the major issues and concerns of a subsequent nationalism in a given population and provide us with clues about the likely growth of a nation and its nationalism. Modern Greece provides an example. Its dual heritage of Byzantine imperial Orthodoxy and classical democratic antiquity shaped the patterns and contents of rival Greek nationalisms in the nineteenth century and beyond – and suggests some reasons for expecting the rise of a powerful nationalism among the Greeks rather than, say, the neighbouring Vlachs.[17]

Third, the approach that I recommend emphasises the important role of memories, values, myths and symbols. Nationalism very often involves the pursuit of 'symbolic' goals – education in a vernacular language, having an own-language TV channel, the preservation of ancient sacred sites like the mosque at Ayodhya or the Wailing Wall area, the right to worship in one's own way, to have one's own courts, schools and press, to wear particular costumes and so on – goals which often bring protest and bloodshed, based as they are on popular memories, symbols and myths. Materialist, rationalist and modernist theories tend to have little to say about these issues, especially the vital component of collective memories.[18] Fourth, an ethno-symbolic approach can help us to understand why nationalism so often has such a widespread popular appeal. The intelligentsia may 'invite the masses into history' and politicise them and their cultures. But why do 'the people' respond? Not simply because of promises of material benefits. Their vernacular culture is now valued and turned into the basis of a new mass culture of the nation. So nationalism often involves the vernacular mobilisation of the masses.[19]

This is why the ethnic form of nationalism has become such a powerful force today. Unlike the civic, territorial nationalism of the French Revolution and the West, which sees the nation as a territorial association of citizens living under the same laws and sharing a mass, public culture, ethnic nationalism regards the nation as a community of genealogical descent, vernacular culture, native history and popular mobilisation. The civic kind of nationalism is a nationalism of order and control, and it suits the existing national states and their dominant ethnies. But it has little to offer the many submerged ethnic minorities incorporated into the older empires and their successor states. So they and their intelligentsia turn to ethnic nationalism and try to reconstruct their community as an ethnic nation. Theirs is the politics of cultural revolt: revolt not only against alien rulers but against 'the fathers', the passive older generations, guardians of ancestral traditions and notables of a traditional order. To achieve their cultural revolution, they must thrust their ethnic communities into the political arena and turn them into political nations. Here is the deeper, inner source of so many ethnic and national conflicts today. The clash of rival nationalisms, ethnic and civic, is at the heart of the conflicts in the Middle East, India, the Caucasus and the Balkans. We can also find it in more muted, but no less persistent, form in the West: in Quebec and Euzkadi, Scotland and Catalonia, Flanders and Corsica, wherever members of marginalised, threatened or aspiring ethnic communities seek to restore their heritage, language and culture.

What follows from this analysis? First, that in a world of political and cultural pluralism, where states and ethnies operate with rival conceptions of the nation and its boundaries, ethno-national conflict is endemic. Second, that nations and nationalisms are a political necessity in a world of competing and unequal states requiring popular legitimation and mobilisation. Third, that because so many people feel their nation performs important social and political functions, it is going to take more than a Maastricht Treaty to wean them away from these deeply-felt national allegiances. And finally, because so many nations are historically embedded in pre-modern ethnic ties, memories and heritages, we are unlikely to witness in our lifetime the transcendence of the nation and the supersession of nationalism – of which so many utopians have dreamt!

NOTES ON CHAPTER 4

1 Professor Anthony Smith is Professor of Politics at the London School of Economics. This paper is based on a lecture given at Warwick University in October 1995 in debate with Prof. Ernest Gellner. Anthony Smith is author of many books, including *The Ethnic Origins of Nations* (Oxford: Blackwell, 1986); *National Identity* (London: Penguin, 1991); *Nationalism and Modernism* (London: Routledge, 1998).
2 Ernest Gellner, *Nations and Nationalism*, (Oxford: Blackwell, 1990 [originally 1983]).
3 A.D. Smith, National Identity (London, Penguin, 1991) chs 1 and 4.
4 See Leonard Tivey, *The Nation State* (New York, St Martin's Press).
5 Charles Tilly, *The Formation of Nation States in Western Europe* (Princeton, Princeton University Press, 1975), Introduction and Conclusion.
6 Walek-Czernecki, 1929; Beryl Tipton, *Conflict and Change* (London, Hutchinson, 1973)
7 Tom Nairn, *The Break-Up of Britain* (London, NLB, 1977) ch. 9
8 Gellner, *Nations and Nationalism, op. cit.*; Benedict Anderson, *Imagined Communities* (London, Verso, 1983).
9 For my own analysis, see A.D. Smith, *Nationalism and Modernism* (London, Routledge, 1988).
10 Eric Hobsbawm and Terence Ranger (eds), *The Invention of Tradition* (Cambridge, Cambridge University Press, 1983), ch. 1.
11 Anderson, *Imagined Communities*, *op. cit.*, ch. 3.
12 A.D. Smith 1995, *Nations and Nationalism in a Global Era* (Cambridge: Polity, 1995), chs 1 and 3.
13 Ernest Gellner, *Nations and Nationalism*, ch. 6.
14 Connor 1984; A.D. Smith 1981, ch. 2.
15 Eric Hobsbawm, *Nations and Nationalism Since 1780* (Cambridge, Cambridge University Press, 1990), ch. 2.
16 See Armstrong 1982; Smith, *The Ethnic Origins of Nations, op. cit.*
17 John Campbell and Phillip Sherrard, Modern Greece (London: Benn, 1968), ch.1; S. Hopffman and P. Kitromilides, *Culture and Society in Contemporary Europe* (London, Allen and Unwin, 1989).
18 See Kapferer 1988; Connor 1993; cf. Tonkin, McDonald and Chapman (eds), *History and Ethnicity* (London: Routledge, 1989).
19 Nairn, *The Break-Up of Britain*, *op. cit.*, ch.2; A.D. Smith, *Social Change* (London: Longman, 1989).

PART III

NATIONAL IDENTITY

5

GENDER, NATIONS AND NATIONALISMS

Catherine Hall[1]

In 1938 the English writer Virginia Woolf asked what the phrase 'our country' meant to a woman. Since women were defined as 'outsiders', in what ways did they belong to the nation? The 'outsider', she continued, pondering on her sense of patriotism, might reflect on the property which her sex owned, how much of England belonged to her, what the law would do for her, what physical protection there was for her. She might conclude that when men insisted on fighting, ostensibly to protect her, what they were doing was satisfying their own 'sex instinct' and procuring benefits which she would not be able to share. As a woman she might feel like saying, 'I have no country. As a woman I want no country. As a woman my country is the whole world.' Woolf's utopian moment of belonging to her sex, beyond nations, speaks across the decades. But it was immediately crosscut with her own ambivalence, her deep sense of being English. For once reason has spoken, she goes on to say, emotion may tug on the heartstrings, 'some love of England dropped into a child's ears by the cawing of rooks in an elm tree, by the splash of waves on a beach, or by English voices murmuring nursery rhymes'. This 'pure, if irrational, emotion' will drive her to secure for England first 'what she desires of peace and freedom for the whole world'.[2]

Woolf's reflections on the eve of the Second World War on the specificities of women's relation to nation, and how different it is in some respects to that of men, reminds us of the gender specifics of national belonging. How is her relation to the nation cross-cut by her sexed self, and how is her sexed self cross-cut by her love of England? Her challenge to us is to understand these forms of gendered belonging, not just at the level of the individual but also as a collective phenomenon. How do women and men identify themselves and become identified as members of a nation? Her thoughts are those of one Englishwoman, long interested in pacifism, responding to the threat of war. But her imagined moment of being an 'outsider' could not survive the war. She heard the bombs, she saw her favourite haunts in Oxford Street and Bloomsbury destroyed, she saw her friends die. There is no way to be outside war, either as a man or a woman.

Virginia Woolf always had an English identity, however complicated. She came from the heartlands, her classed self secure. Yet for innumerable women and men this is not the case. There is no nation to belong to: they are 'outsiders' of another kind, migrants, asylum seekers, members of national liberation movements. We cannot assume either women's or men's relation to nations or nationalisms: it is something about which we need to ask questions, seek answers. We live in a world rent by national and ethnic conflict, conflict which often takes gendered forms. Rape, for example, has been used by all sides as an 'instrument of war' in the former Yugoslavia.[3] There could be no clearer example of the ways in which gender relations are a site upon which ethnic and national conflicts are played out.

Yet most of the analysis of nations and nationalisms pays no attention to questions of gender. Nationalisms are interpreted, for example, as part of the anti-colonial project; as the politicised expression of particular groups of historically specific people; as forms of cultural belonging to imagined communities; as homogenising or differentiating discourses which aim their appeal at people presumed to have certain things in common and against those who are seen as different; as articulating class or ethnic forms of belonging. Alongside this work, however, a fast-growing literature is now emerging which suggests that there is an important element missing in traditional accounts of nations and nationalisms. It argues that gender is constitutive of both. In this short essay I want to draw attention to these arguments, first developed by feminists, and suggest that analyses of nations and nationalisms which do not take gender into account cannot give us an adequate picture of how nations are constructed or nationalisms rooted in the political and emotional lives of men and women. My argument is that the processes and activities connected with nations and nationalisms, the political, economic and cultural ways in which nations are imagined, challenged and understood have to be grasped through the lens of gender, as well as those of 'race', ethnicity and class.

Woolf knew that her nation was England with its distinctive landscape, sounds and nursery rhymes. That she loved. Its formal nationhood, however, its property laws and its legal processes were what constituted women – including her, a white upper-middle-class educated woman – as 'outsiders', excluded from full citizenship. The issue of who belongs to a nation and in what ways, who are citizens and who are subjects, is one which is never concluded, for the process of nation formation is indeed that, a process. Nations are not made once and for ever. Rather they are constantly re-made and re-imagined, the boundaries redrawn. In Britain, for example, the two great Reform Acts of the nineteenth century, those of 1832 and 1867, marked moments at which the meaning of citizenship significantly changed.[4] First large numbers of middle-class men and then large numbers of working-class men were granted the right to vote, to not only carry arms for their country but also play a part in the election of their representatives. The Reform Act of 1867 effected a reconstitution of the nation – it was the moment at which between 35 and 40% of the adult male working class was enfranchised and, as Keith McClelland has recently argued, a new subject constituted, the working-class male citizen.[5] The debates of 1866–7, which took place inside and outside parliament, were concerned with different ways of belonging to nation and empire, who were subjects and who were citizens, and what the hierarchies were within those categories. Class, 'race', ethnicity and gender were all crucially in play in these debates, and provided the lines along which boundaries could be drawn up, different social groups included or excluded from the imagined community of the nation – both in its political definition, those who are citizens, and what might be described in Sarah Benton's term as its familial definition, those who are born into it and are subject to it.[6] But the debates over nation do not make sense unless the extent to which they were framed by the empire is recognised, for it was impossible to think about the 'mother country' and its specificities without reference to the colonies. The colonies provided the many benchmarks which allowed the English to determine what they did not want to be and who they thought they were. Through the construction of imagined others in Australia, in Ireland, in Canada, in New Zealand, in the ex-colony of America, and most significantly in 1866–7 in Jamaica, the English reached a settlement as to who was to belong to the new nation.

It was respectable working men who were deemed to be ready for inclusion in the body politic. Two years of debate took place over precisely which British men should be 'given' the franchise, debate which was always framed by the political mobilisation of the Reform League. Enormous demonstrations of men took place in the months preceding the passing of the act, reminding those in parliament of other forms of power. Gladstone, the Liberal leader, had come to the conclusion that working men had earned the right to vote, had shown their maturity during the American Civil War, when large numbers of them had proved their willingness to put a cause that they believed in, the triumph of the North and the abolition of slavery, before their own material interests. Gladstone's interest was in where the line was to be drawn in the new system of suffrage: which men included, which excluded. Those lines were constructed around particular notions of respectable masculinity and its central virtue, independence. The men who could vote were those who had homes, those who had families, those who had regular employment. Excluded were those who were not settled, vagrants and wanderers – which often meant the Irish – men with no fixed address and no secure work. It was independence which gave some working-class men the status to become part of the gendered world of the political nation, members of the fraternity of England, privy to the rational discourse of politics, freed from the sphere of passion and emotion which was intimately linked to the status of dependant. Such men would not threaten the fabric of the national culture, would not 'make us any less English, or less national than we now are'.[7] But women, who should be dependants, would threaten that national culture if they were enfranchised.

At the same time that the question of which men to enfranchise was so exhaustively discussed, the issue of women's right to vote was also raised. In 1832, it had been formally clarified for the first time that women could not vote. By 1867, women's suffrage had been an important issue for feminist groups for a long time, for it was clear that the vote was the symbolic crux of citizenship. A petition was organised seeking the vote for women on the same terms as men, and John Stuart Mill raised the subject in the House of Commons on their behalf.[8] The result was a brief debate and a speedy dismissal of the issue. Women, the House of Commons concluded, were certainly not citizens, they were subjects. They were excluded from the suffrage because they were women, 'naturally' gentle and affectionate, the guardians of domesticity and morality, not suited to participation in the public world of politics.

The thinking around the domestic franchise was framed by imperial concerns and by assumptions as to what was politically appropriate in countries at different stages of 'civilisation'. In November 1865, a rebellion had erupted at Morant Bay in Jamaica. Jamaica had been colonised by the British in 1655 and granted representative government shortly afterwards. The island had its own House of Assembly, dominated by white property owners, and was responsible for its own legislation and finance, subject to the crown as represented by the Governor. The Governor in 1865, responded violently to the rebellion, convinced – as were the vast majority of the white population on the island – that black people meant to massacre them all. British troops were brought in, and draconian punishments meted out. The result was a public outcry in Britain, and a Royal Commission on Jamaica. Early in 1866, however, the British parliament was entirely willing to go along with the Jamaican House of Assembly's abolition of itself and of representative government on the island. Jamaican representative government had long been criticised as unsatisfactory both by the majority black population, and its supporters, and by the Colonial Office, which was contemptuous of the white planter mentality. In the aftermath of Morant Bay, the planters, who had previously strenuously defended their right to self-government, preferred to accept crown colony status and rule from London rather than making concessions to democratic – which meant coloured and black – rule. In the House of Commons, no-one was interested in defending the principle of representative government in Jamaica, for the majority population had only recently emerged from slavery and come under 'civilising influences'. They were seen as not yet fit for liberty. Black men were clearly not ready to constitute a body politic, Jamaica was a colony, not a nation.

Critical moments in the construction of the British nation, I am suggesting, cannot be made sense of outside the gendered and colonial context. Members of Parliament debated Jamaica alongside women's suffrage and men's suffrage – it was all part of a related discussion, and 'nation' derived its particular and concrete meanings from 'empire'. For what did it mean to be English outside the notions of white superiority which were premised upon colonised and non-white bodies? Nation, in other words, is constituted through processes of inclusion and exclusion which in this instance depended on the boundaries drawn through gender, class and 'race'.

Other scholars have demonstrated these processes at work. Nancy Leys Stepan, for example, in her book on the eugenics movement in Latin America investigates the particular meanings of eugenics in the Catholic, post-colonial societies of Brazil,

Mexico and Argentina in the 1920s and 1930s, when new nations were being constituted out of heterogeneous populations. Eugenicists played a part in structuring notions of inclusion and exclusion in national bodies, giving that body its ethnic and gendered identity.[9] Through eugenics, she argues, 'gender and race were tied to the politics of national identity'. Reproductive rights became part of ethnic and national strategies. To take other examples, Carroll Smith-Rosenberg has narrated the place of the racialised and gendered other in the making of the American Republic;[10] Meera Kosambi has demonstrated how religion, ethnicity and gender all became vital to the state in defining who belonged to the Indian nation;[11] and Marilyn Lake has written on the particular forms of masculinity which underpinned the Australian nation from its inception.[12] This body of work has initiated lively debate.

Woolf's sense of herself in relation to the political nation is, as we have seen, that of an 'outsider', albeit an extremely privileged one. But her sense of cultural belonging – the cawing of the rooks in an elm tree, the splash of waves on a beach, English voices murmuring nursery rhymes – is linked to childhood and landscape. I want to argue that these forms of cultural belonging are also profoundly gendered. Let me take an example from Jamaica, a place which was not recognised as a political nation, with full independence, until 1962. The case for the abolition of slavery had been made on the basis that it would be possible to create a successful free labour economy in colonies such as Jamaica: that the end of slavery, far from resulting in a return to barbarism, as the planters argued, would open the way to a new civilisation. After full emancipation, in 1838, the problem which preoccupied the chief representatives of the abolitionists, the missionaries, was how to create a new society which would cut the links with both slavery and Africa – both identified for them with different forms of barbarism. The missionaries worked to build a new moral world, one to which newly freed African men and women would feel deep attachment and belonging, a physical belonging which would re-work their relation to Africa, a cultural belonging which would mark them as new Christian subjects, the black Christian man and the black Christian woman, of the British Empire. Emancipation had given enslaved men and women their political, economic and social freedom. Conversion gave them a new life in Christ, the possibility to be born anew.[13]

The missionary dream of this new Jerusalem depended on new villages with a new gender order. The villages were designed with the chapel and mission-house at the centre, surrounded by neat cottages, occupied by proper Christian families. The sexual depravities of slavery would be forgotten, marriages encouraged, family life celebrated. Neat white-washed cottages would become places of happiness and nurseries of piety. Men were urged to act as men, to be independent, to recognise the dignity of labour, to command their wives to stay at home and look after the children. Real freedom depended on the ownership of houses, which prevented prying planters from charging exorbitant rents or treating tenants in unmanly ways. Every man should be free to sit under his own vine or fig-tree, to call his wife and his children his own. Women should abandon their gaudy dress and appear modestly clad, their success no longer dependent on the favours of lascivious owners but on their industrious husbands and their own domestic management. The men would work on the estates and grow food for their families, the women would look after the homes and gardens, and bring up their children to love, honour and obey. These new villages, many of them named after eminent abolitionists, would provide the imagined landscapes of the new Jamaica, would shape the forms of cultural belonging of the next generations. The missionary dream was indeed a dream, for it refused to recognise the African legacy, and tried to wipe clean those histories. It was doomed to failure, but it has left its mark on the Jamaican imagination and on the gendered forms of national belonging which have survived into the present.

Gender issues around nation and nationalism are perhaps most sharply articulated during periods of military conflict, when men's and women's bodies become the site of that conflict. As many have noted, the masculinisation of war and of citizenship are intimately connected, and the exclusion of women from the military has been a key aspect of their exclusion from citizenship. Cynthia Enloe, in her work on militarism, notes the strategic importance of women's sexuality, together with their reproductive and child-rearing roles, in emerging nationalisms, and considers the control which nation-states attempt to exert over their women and girls in their efforts to protect, revive and create nations. She asks how national identities become militarised, a question which Sarah Benton addresses in relation to Ireland at the beginning of the twentieth century. Manliness, she argues, was the key public virtue in both America and Britain, and it allowed a man to claim possession of himself, a nation to claim possession of itself.

> An army was the means of marshalling a mass of people for regeneration. The symbol of a nation's preparedness to take control of its own soul was the readiness to bear arms... The ideal form of relationship in war is the brotherhood, both as actuality and potent myth.[14]

Pat Barker's brilliant trilogy is an evocation of some of the complexity of the meanings of war for men, around violence, pain, love and death.[15]

The issue of sexual violence and its use as a weapon of war has necessarily been taken up in the aftermath of the conflicts in the former Yugoslavia. While rape has long been utilised in war, it is only now with the public attention given to questions of sexual violence and sexual abuse that it is being openly recognised and discussed. Atina Grossmann, in her analysis of the rape of German women by the Red Army on the eastern front during the closing weeks of World War Two, argues persuasively that we must historicise our understandings of rape, and that it has different meanings in different contexts.[16] As Elaine Scarry explicates, the logic of war is to destroy your enemy, not just politically and economically, but culturally and psychically as well. This means destroying people's identities, who they are and how they perceive themselves. Rape can be a potent weapon in such a strategy.[17] Renata Salecl pushes this argument further and suggests that the aim of war is to destroy the fantasy structure of a whole population.[18] National myths are constructed about certain territories which become sacred, symbolic of the nation's existence. The destruction of the fantasy of the nation occurs through inflicting real injuries on bodies. The aim of rape is to shatter the fantasy structure of an individual and to attack the masculinity of the victim's fathers, husbands and brothers, for they have failed in their responsibility to protect 'their women', a potent source of national feeling. The aim of war more generally is to rape the enemy's 'motherland', the body of the community, the body politic.

In 1989, Floya Anthias and Nira Yuval-Davis theorised the relation between woman, the nation and the state. They argued that women are crucially present in national processes as biological, cultural, ethnic and symbolic reproducers of the nation.[19] Some feminist scholars have focused on this symbolic question, arguing that women act as markers of an ethnic group's cultural identity or as carriers and reproducers of 'authentic' traditions.[20] Deniz Kandyoti, for example, has looked at nationalist movements in the Middle East and the issue of female emancipation as a mark of 'modernisation', concluding that women continue to bear and reproduce national traditions and the idea of the 'authentic' nation.[21] Aihwa Ong, on the other hand, reminds us that no-one should assume that women's interests are not necessarily represented in nationalist movements, or that women are always the passive victims of Islamic nationalist movements. In Malaysia, as she shows, women have capitalised on their moral power as symbols of cultural authenticity to renegotiate their relations with men.[22] In India, to take another example, Hindu fundamentalists have re-worked traditional notions of womanhood, which have long been central to certain varieties of Indian nationalism, and succeeded in mobilising large numbers of women to the belief in the possibility of a new religious state. The communal violence which characterises India in the 1990s has brought with it increasing violence against women in the form of dowry deaths, sati and the use of amniocentesis as a way of limiting the numbers of female children. Hindu fundamentalists have drawn on a rich and gendered mythology. Their call to arms against the enemy, Islam, is in defence of the motherland and the purity of its women: they are the boundary keepers, the bearers of tradition, but also potentially the enemy within who must be kept under supervision.[23]

What then of the complex relation between nationalisms and feminisms? Virginia Woolf, living in an old country which had never had to wage an anti-colonial struggle internally, grew up with a particular kind of feminism, linked to a transformative politics but not to a movement for national emancipation. But many feminisms have emerged in the context of liberation movements and have had complex relations to those politics. While in some instances feminisms have been able to achieve gains for women through their involvement with national organisations, at other times they have been compelled to put aside questions of women's rights in the name of the larger struggle. In some instances, the 'woman question' has been vital to the founding of new nations, as, for example, in Egypt.[24] Similarly, gender and sexuality played a crucial part in the national liberation and modernisation struggles in Iran, as Joanna de Groot has shown.[25] On occasion, women have been able to engage with nationalist struggles in such a way as to secure further rights, in other contexts the outcome has been less benevolent. Clearly there is no necessary connection between feminism and nationalism, and indeed nationalisms have often been anti-feminist, as we can see in the current triumph of Islamic fundamentalists in Afghanistan.

An understanding of the relation between feminism and nationalism depends on historical specificity. There are no givens, only the articulation in particular historical conjectures of political discourses, movements and peoples. Virginia Woolf's question, what does 'our country' mean to a woman and how is that different from what it means to a man, reverberates in the present. We are beginning to have some answers, but there are many more questions to be asked. They do seem worth asking.

NOTES ON CHAPTER 5

1 Catherine Hall is Professor of History at the University College London. She is author of *White, Male and Middle Class: Explorations in Feminism and History* (Cambridge: Polity, 1992) and *Family Fortunes: Men and Women of the English Middle Class, 1980–1850* (with Leonore Davidoff) (London: Routledge, 1992).

She writes: 'My thinking on this subject benefited greatly from the workshop "Gender and Nationalism" organised by the Central European University Project on Gender and Culture at the University of Essex in November 1995. The discussion which took place after the Warwick debate at which a version of this paper was presented was also helpful in making me clarify my own arguments.'

2 Virginia Woolf, *Three Guineas*, ed. Michele Barrett, (Harmondsworth: Penguin, 1993), p 234.

3 Bette Dernich, 'Of Arms, Men, and Ethnic War in (Former) Yugoslavia', in Constance R. Sutton (ed.), *Feminism, Nationalism and Militarism* (New York: Association for Feminist Anthropology, 1995).

4 For a longer version of this argument about 1867 see Catherine Hall, 'Rethinking Imperial Histories: The Reform Act of 1867', *New Left Review* 208, Nov/Dec 1994.

5 Keith McClelland, 'Rational and Respectable Men: Rethinking the 1867 Reform Act' in Laura Frader and Sonia Rose (eds), *Gender and Working-Class Formation in Modern Europe* (Ithaca: Cornell University Press, 1996).

6 Sarah Benton, 'Manliness, Militias and Making the Nation', unpublished paper, October 1992.

7 R.H. Hutton, 'The Political Character of the Working Class' in *Essays on Reform* (London: Macmillan, 1867), p 36.

8 For a fascinating account of feminist thinking on citizenship and civilisation at this time see Jane Rendall, 'Citizenship, Culture and Civilisation: the languages of British suffragists 1866–74' in Melanie Nolan and Caroline Daley (eds), *Suffrage and Beyond: International Feminist Perspectives* (Auckland University Press, Auckland, 1994).

9 Nancy Leys Stepan, 'The Hour of Eugenics' in *Race, Gender and Nation in Latin America* (Ithaca: Cornell University Press, 1991), p 105.

10 Carroll Smith-Rosenberg, 'Captured Subjects/Savage Others: Violently Engendering the New American', *Gender and History* 5, Summer 1993.

11 Meera Kosambi, 'An Uneasy Intersection: Gender, Ethnicity and Crosscutting Identities in India', *Social Politics*, Summer 1995.

12 See, for example, Marilyn Lake, 'Mission Impossible: How Men Gave Birth to the Australian Nation – Nationalism, Gender and Other Seminal Acts', *Gender and History*, vol. 4, no. 3, Autumn 1992.

13 For a longer exploration of this moment see Catherine Hall, 'White Visions, Black Lives: the Free Villages of Jamaica', *History Workshop* 36, Autumn 1993.

14 Sarah Benton, 'Women Disarmed: The militarisation of politics in Ireland 1913–23', *Feminist Review* 50, Summer 1995, p 148.
15 Pat Barker, *Regeneration, The Eye in the Door, The Ghost Road* (Harmondsworth: Penguin, 1996).
16 Atina Grossmann, 'A Question of Silence: the rape of German women by Occupation soldiers', *October* 72, Spring 1995.
17 Elaine Scarry, source unknown.
18 Renata Salecl, 'The Fantasy Structure of Nationalist Discourse', source unknown.
19 Floya Anthias and Nira Yuval-Davis (eds), *Woman-Nation-State* (Macmillan, London, 1989), 'Introduction'.
20 See the special issue of *Women's Studies International Forum* on 'Gender, Ethnicity and Nationalism' (ed. Barbara Einhorn), 18, (5/6), 1995.
21 Deniz Kandyoti, 'Identity and its Discontents: Women and the Nation', *Millennium: Journal of International Studies* 20, 1991.
22 Aihwa Ong, 'Postcolonial Nationalism: Women and Retraditionalisation in the Islamic Imaginary, Malaysia' in Sutton (ed.), *Feminism, Nationalism, and Militarism, op. cit.*
23 Eva Friedlander, 'Inclusive Boundaries, Exclusive Ideologies: Hindu Fundamentalism and Gender in India Today', in Sutton (ed.), *Feminism, Nationalism, and Militarism, op. cit*; Sucheta Mazumdar, 'Women on the March: Right-Wing Mobilisation in Contemporary India', *Feminist Review* 49, Spring 1995.
24 Margot Badran, *Feminists, Islam and Nation: Gender and the Making of Modern Egypt* (Princeton: Princeton University Press, 1993).
25 Joanna de Groot, 'The Dialectics of Gender: Women, Men and Political Discourses in Iran c.1890–1930', *Gender and History* vol. 5, no. 2, Summer 1993.

6

THE ELUSIVE CULTURAL COMMUNITY

Olivier Roy[1]

INTRODUCTION

We tend to see culture as a relatively homogeneous set of common patterns defining a community (language, religion, family relations, diet etc) wrapped into the sense of a common identity. Of course 'culturalists' do not ignore the transformations that history and social changes might bring to such a community, but they tend to consider that at a given time there is such a thing as a 'cultural community'. Societies become multicultural in the sense that they are made of a collection of various 'cultures'. In most societies, according to the 'multiculturalist' approach, there is a dominant, even hegemonic, culture and a cluster of minority groups. The question is then to retain the concept of a common polity while making room for the different cultures.

The other approach considers that a polity is made of citizens, not of communities, and that the state should not deal with groups but with the citizens themselves. This is supposed to be the 'French syndrome' inherited from the 'Jacobin' state. The main criticism of this approach is that it allows the dominant culture to impose its standards in the name of an abstract citizen who is a legal fiction. The dominant group wraps itself into the cloak of universalism and ignores the fact that any 'abstract citizen' also belongs to a specific culture.

My own position is not so much to support the 'Jacobin' concept of a direct and unmediated relation between abstract citizens and the state, as to show that the idea of a Western society made of a collection of different 'cultural communities' does not make sense: not because the cultural factor in itself is irrelevant but because it does not allow one to define communities. The cultural factor should be introduced into political science, but not into law because it is elusive and transitional. In 'multiculturalism' we should drop 'culturalism' but keep the 'multi'.

First of all, the notion of a 'cultural community' varies too much both in time and in space. What is there in common between the problematics of cultural diversity among Tamils and Sinhalese in Sri Lanka and in Great Britain? Both will be seen in this distant country as sharing the same 'Asian culture', while the question of 'multiculturalism' will arise in their common relationship with the now dominant cultural group (the so-called 'whites'). The question of the relations of Hungarians and Romanians in Transylvania cannot be thought of in the same terms as the relations of Muslims and 'Christians' in Great Britain or France. The link with land, history and language has nothing to do with it. To speak in terms of 'minority' versus 'majority' implies some symmetry in what defines both groups. This symmetry does not exist, and cannot exist if we refer to 'multiculturalism' in Western Europe.

One definitively cannot use the same intellectual tools when speaking of pristine identities and imported identities, not only because the problematic of relations between various cultures changes, but also because the very nature of the 'cultures' undergoes a deep evolution in the immigration process. This is not only a question of spatial movement but also of time: what defines the 'Muslim Indian' identity is rather different for a first-generation immigrant and for his grandson who does not speak Urdu. We are confronted here with transitional identities. This does not necessarily imply that we are heading towards full integration into the 'dominant' group, but that we cannot base our analysis on relatively well defined 'minority groups'.

Of course, a common sense of identity might remain both in time and space, but it is no more than a 'nominal ethnicity' dealing with a changing and elusive content, which is more determined by social markers than by strictly cultural patterns. Moreover, even the divide between nominal 'ethnic groups' is not pristine but imposed by the country of residence. 'Asians',

'Blacks' and even 'Muslims' are not pristine, but reconstructed identities which refer to different people in the USA (where one speaks of 'ethnic groups') and in Great Britain (where one speaks of 'races'). People originating from the Indian sub-continent will not be classified the same way in both countries. Interestingly enough, the minority groups usually fight to be recognised positively along the patterns prevailing in the country of residence. See, for example, the successful endeavours of South Asians not to be classified as 'blacks' by US immigration law, while they accept the status of 'non-white' under the legal perception of 'racial relations' in Great Britain, and while it would be unlawful in France to classify people by 'race'.[2] New categories appear: 'Asians' in Great Britain (rather different from Asians in USA or France, where it means people from the Far East), but also 'Muslims' (in which case religious identity is built above ethnic affiliations). Actually operating identities in the contemporary West are thus nominal or metaphorical, with less and less relation to pristine identities.

My last point addresses the question how is it possible to recognise and give a legal status to identities which are thus reconstructed and transitional? Such a move is not only based on wrong premises, but it might become a limit to individual freedom and to the normal processes of social change. Ecology is good for whales, not for societies. If cultural identity is based on free choice, it will remain elusive, dynamic and thus difficult to embody in the law. If it is imposed by the law (which would be a consequence of any policy of affirmative action), it will fix borders between groups, and in some cases might give fewer rights to certain categories of citizens (for example women, if the state agrees, as does secular India, to include some *shariat* principles into personal status).

I will focus here on the problematic of multicultural societies in Western countries, because it is the place where the paradigm of multiculturalism as a universal concept came into discussion.

FROM PRISTINE ETHNIC CULTURE TO A METAPHORICAL ETHNICITY

There is no such thing as a set of different ethnic cultures co-existing in Western Europe, whether native or immigrant. History, land and language shape not only a 'culture' but the relations, or more precisely the concept of the relations between different 'cultures'. Relations between the French central 'Jacobin' state and the Bretons have little to do with relations between the also central and 'Jacobin' Turkish state and the

Kurds. One among many differences is that the linguistic 'francisation' has been done in Bretagne, as elsewhere in France, by local elites and not by authoritarian state policy; thus when public general instruction was imposed in 1881, urban elites were already French-speaking and all the local schoolteachers were 'natives'. We can of course speak of a 'Breton culture' in a rather vague sense, but this could not be insulated and defined by a set of clear patterns (language, for example). It is more a question of personal experience and of the dynamic and multiple ways of referring to the external world.

In fact the question of multiculturalism has arisen in Europe, since the sixties, through the sudden and massive influx of millions of immigrants from the Third World. These immigrants had, for the most part (but not in all cases), a very different background of culture, languages and religion. When it became clear that they were here to stay, and that full integration was not an easy and smooth process, a debate arose on how to cope with the problem. Three attitudes might summarise the debate: rejectionism ('let's preserve our identity'), assimilationism ('let the immigrants become full members of the dominant model') or multiculturalism ('let us accept the co-existence of different cultures in the same polity'). But these three attitudes are all based on the wrong assumption that there are given, relatively permanent and clearly demarcated cultural identities.

The first generation of immigrants used to come with a pristine 'ethnic culture' (language, customs, religion, family patterns, diet, music etc). In these cultures the different circles of identity (parochial, ethnic, national, religious) were not perceived as antagonist levels: identity was 'experienced' as a whole. Nevertheless, in the process of immigration these different levels might come into conflict. Collective identities have to be recomposed, even reinvented, because personal experience no more fits with the largest group to which the individual is supposed to belong. Even at the level of pristine and imported identity, reconstruction – or at least a multi-level approach – has been under way. During the war between West and East Pakistan in 1971, antagonism was strong between Bangladeshis and Pakistanis living in Great Britain, but both defended a common Muslim identity when it came to educational issues. National and religious identities, which did not conflict in the pristine cultures, were experienced as two different levels of identification in the immigrant universe.

Are the migrants from the Algerian Great Kabylie, who settled in Paris during the 1950s, Kabyles, Algerians, North Africans or Arabs? It depends on the context. On the political scene they massively chose to be Algerians during the 1954–62 war of liberation. Such a turn, made sometimes at a high cost, shows that identity is a choice, and more specifically a political one. But the Kabyles always stressed their Kabyle specificity (better integration, a more secular mind, a disdain for Arabic and a closer knit of parochial and familial networks), which contradicted the official Algerian nationalism based on an Arabo-Islamic identity. The same individual might at different time and place stress one of the elements of such a set of multiple identities without seeing any contradiction for him or herself. But when we come to define groups, such a dynamic flexibility ceases to work. The fact of immigration creates distinction between different identities which were not seen as different in the country of origin; in particular, it creates a choice between a smaller identity, tribal or parochial, which is usually the effective one in matrimonial and business relationships (as in the case of Bangladeshis from Syhlet in Great Britain), and a larger one, based either on citizenship (Bangladeshi, Pakistani) or on religion (Muslims).

Frequent polemics emerge among the concerned groups: who is a 'true' something (be it Pakistani, Muslim, Asian etc)? Should one associate along 'ethnic', national or religious lines, these three levels being no more in tune? Philip Lewis mentions, for example, the breaking up of an 'ethnic' association, the Asian Youth Movement, along religious lines: 'AYM did not survive the return in the late 1980s to community consolidations around separate Hindu, Sikh and Muslim identity'.[3] This case exemplifies the problem: cultural identity in immigration is a matter of choice and strategy, not of pristine culture. The Asian Youth Movement had been founded on an anti-racist, 'third-world' line, before it split into non-symmetric communal groups. Sikhs opposed Hindus on the question of 'Khalistan', ie on an ethnic-nationalist basis. Hindus in this case saw themselves not as an ethnic group, and not even so much as a religious group, but as supporters of India which is a multi-ethnic and secular state. Muslims, though originating from the Indian sub-continent, did not pretend to be 'Pakistanis' or to oppose Hindus on an ethnic basis, like the Sikhs, but saw themselves as part of a universal, world-wide, non-ethnic community based solely on the tenets of religion. Indian Muslims in Great Britain will associate with Arabs and converts, which is nonsense for Sikhs and Hindus. There is no symmetry between the three groups on the British political scene, although there is one in India (all are communal groups where religion is a marker of ethnicity).

In any event, these pristine cultures, already reshaped by the simple fact of settling abroad, soon became elusive with the second and third generations. Language, clothes, patterns of entertainment and, sooner or later, patterns of marriage change. One shifts from Urdu to English, from Algerian Arabic to French.

One ceases to eat couscous in favour of MacDonalds. Parochial and familial connections ease in favour of larger groupings. Fewer brides come from the village of origin (and not only because of restrictions in immigration laws). Patterns of authority also change: traditional elders give way to more successful youth (either in business, education or politics). New customs make their way in, possibly borrowed or adapted from elsewhere.

Nevertheless, acculturation does not necessarily mean that at some time (earlier in France than in Great Britain or Germany) the new generations always join the mainstream culture. What appear are different kind of reconstructed identities. We do not get rid of 'ethnicity', but the problem is to define the content under such a label, and to see to what extent we can speak of a culture. First, we have already seen that 'ethnic' denominations are reconstructed in the countries of immigration: 'Asian' does not correspond to a pristine ethnic culture in which Hindus and Muslims see each other as different, if not antagonist, cultures, whereas they are included in the same grouping in Great Britain. But there are also interesting cases of invention of an ethnic category, where the 'ethnic' markers are in fact purely social and generational: the term 'beur' in France (feminine 'beurette'), which is non-derogatory slang for 'Arab', designates French-speaking youngsters of Arab descent living in poor suburbs. Of the three markers which make a 'beur' (generational, social and familial), only the last has something to do with 'ethnicity', and there is no ethnic culture at all. The 'beur' culture is a western, urban, youth sub-culture, comparable to that of the American Blacks of the ghettos. Dress (base-ball caps), diet (Mac'Do), music ('ra'ï'), language (a French slang called 'verlan' or 'reverse'), have nothing to do with Arab ethnic culture (except ra'ï, which is a mix of western and Arab popular music). Both the first generation and the 'true believers' see this 'culture' as alien and westernised. In a very logical way, the few 'beurs' who become 'born again Muslims' give up this denomination, as well as 'Arab', in favour of a purely 'Muslim' identity. The problem is that any endeavour to 'return' to a more authentic culture is necessarily based on a reconstructed identity, in this case, as we shall see, that of the 'true Islam'.

The fact that nominal ethnic identities are more and more reshaped along social patterns, at least among the socially excluded, tends to give it a political content. We are witnessing the rebuilding of a protest identity among a sector of the second and third generation, using not the pristine cultures but ideological slogans which originated from leftist Western traditions. Here ethnic labels are reinterpreted in social and political terms. During the Gulf War, many immigrants' children rallied under the banner of anti-war movements, protesting against the 'new world order' that underlay the crusade against Saddam Hussein. There is a conjunction between a space of social exclusion, that of the former working class, and a new ethnic label. There is a continuity between anti-racist, leftist and protest movements of the seventies on one hand, and the anti-hegemonic, Third World 'multiculturalist' movements of today, where in fact Third World is no more a geographic and economic concept but rather a socio-cultural one. This continuity is more obvious in Great Britain where a part of the Labour movement supports the multiculturalist approach, than in France, where the secular ideology of the left entails some reluctance to support what is seen as a religious affirmation (an obvious prejudice during the so-called 'scarf affair'). But the recent terrorist actions in France show that far from being 'imported', this radicalisation is the direct heir of older ultra-leftist movements such as 'Action directe' (which was dismantled in the mid-eighties). Far from being imported, the politicisation of 'ethnic' groups follows the political traditions of the countries of settlement, for better or for worse. Ethnic labels and slogans are new, but they do not really alter the political scene, precisely because they mobilise on social rather than cultural problems.

FROM RELIGIOUS TO ETHNIC COMMUNITY... AND BACK

In France, as in Great Britain, the only movement able to challenge the state on the multicultural issue is not an ethnic movement but a religious one, Islam. In Great Britain, this is shown by the call for the application of the blasphemy law in favour of Islam, and in France by the demand that Muslim girls be permitted to wear scarves inside classrooms. This is quite coherent. We saw that ethnicity is transitional and metaphorical, and cannot offer the basis for political action, because it lacks any stable constituency. Religion, on the other hand, can offer a set of stable and unambivalent principles, the observance of which could define a 'community'. But, paradoxically, the emergence of a Muslim community is the perfect example of a reconstructed community.

The endeavour to build a community whose sole criteria is religious faith supposes precisely the negation of any specific culture and ethnicity. This is explicit in the declarations and preachings of most religious leaders, and was the cornerstone of the acceptance of 'black Muslims' in the USA by mainstream Islamic clerics.[4] In this sense, Islam is not only what the different Muslim ethnic groups have in common, but is also what should appeal to 'whites'. The new Muslim leaders in the countries of immigration base their action on an Islamic reformism, and sometimes an Islamic fundamentalism, by labelling as 'un-Islamic' many customs and habits from the pristine cultures, or at least by distancing themselves from traditionalism. They advocate the use of the language of the new country, which is now the universal language. Through this contribution to the de-legitimisation of pristine cultures, Islamic reformism or fundamentalism becomes part of the process of acculturation even as it offers a substitute identity.

In fact, Islam has always been entangled with some specific cultures, but Islam is not a culture *per se*: it is a set of beliefs and rituals which defines a code. There are Muslim cultures, but not an Islamic culture. A Punjabi ballet makes sense, not an Islamic ballet. There is no 'Islamic novel', Islamic sports, Islamic entertainment etc, but only some moral precepts that could apply to any field of activities. All the endeavours of the Islamic reformists, and especially the fundamentalists, have been to distinguish Islam from other practices which, even when not forbidden, are not Islam. Reconstruction means a break from the pristine cultures in order to assess and stress the universality of the purely religious message. Hence there are two possibilities for a true believer: either to accept the dominant culture to the extent that it fits with the tenets of the religion, or to shed away everything which is 'un-Islamic' and live in an autarchic counter-society, closer to a sect than to a community.

The strength of the religious Islamic call among sons of immigrants is not a call for authenticity, a return to a lost pristine culture, but the invention of a new identity. Traditional Islam, as embodied in pristine cultures, has little to offer to shape this new identity which has to cope with the challenge of 'de-territorialisation'. Islam is no more associated with a specific space, 'dar-ul islam', where Muslims live under Muslim rulers. To think of Islam as a minority group entails more than a few adjustments with 14 centuries of history.

Religion allows one to start from nothing: it is a code, not a culture; one can learn to be a believer, using any language and living in any society. Religion is now the marker of a new invented 'ethnicity', void of culture, but expressing a reconstructed identity in search of recognition.

If Islam is a part of many ethnic cultures, nobody could be called an 'ethnic' Muslim. The paradox is that Islam tends to be seen as an ethnic marker in Western society, as if Muslims were members of some specific new ethnic group. The confusion between ethnicity (not to speak about 'race') and religion is particularly worrying, because it negates the basis of almost any religion, and specifically of Islam: the claim to be universal. To consider 'Muslims' as a quasi-ethnic group is the best way to negate them as 'believers'. But we are anyway far from the question of multiculturalism.

INDIVIDUAL CHOICE VERSUS COMMUNITY RIGHTS: THE RIGHT NOT TO BELONG

The official recognition of different cultural communities entails two problems.

First, if we are right in our assessment that there are no given cultures to be recognised as such, any official recognition of a culture, or of an 'ethnic community' by the state means that such an entity is more a legal fiction than a social reality. What is called a culture here is a kind of snap-shot taken from a complex reality, immediately frozen and perpetuated by a legal definition. Defining cultures means to freeze a process of multiple and changing identities. It is not applicable, because the discrepancy between the legal definition and the social process will grow.

Second, such a policy will impinge on individual freedom not so much by preventing choices as by making choice compulsory. Why should one be obliged to answer to the question, who are you? In fact, the space between authorising and making compulsory is narrow, because of the pressure from the communalist militants to abide with what defines the community.

A good example is the 'scarf affair' in France, which arose from the prohibition against wearing headscarves in classrooms (not in schools as such, as it has sometimes been said). The actors wanted not only to gain the right to choose, but also the legal recognition of woman's scarf as a marker of a communal identity, thus making it a moral obligation for any girl calling herself Muslim to wear the scarf. What we might term 'communalisation' is not so much a grass-root demand (there have been relatively few cases out of a population of tens of thousands of 'Muslim' schoolgirls) as a strategy of a communal elite of would-be notables. Such pressure impinges on the freedom of Muslim girls who do not wish to face the choice: either I wear the scarf or I might be considered as a bad Muslim by the most militant part of the community.

The phenomenon is also apparent in Great Britain: some self-proclaimed leaders claim to represent the demands of a Muslim community, ask for a recognition by the state of this community and, if successful, almost automatically get the right to 'represent' it. The community is created by this, as it is defined by its potential leaders; its creation does not necessarily express the will of its would-be members.

One solution would be to recognise communities only to the extent they are based on personal choice. This is certainly more democratic, but destroys the case for multiculturalism. A culture is not a choice (and not a given fact either). In this sense there is no more 'multiculturalism' nor 'minority rights', but a collection of individuals some of whom willingly join a community. But freedom supposes also the right to leave. This neither fits the definition of an ethnic group (what about the free choice of one's ethnicity?) nor the way some religious groups see the question of membership. For most Islamic scholars, to be a Muslim is a choice only for the convert. The path is thus narrow between allowing the scarf and making it compulsory for those who are, or are said by their parents to be, Muslim. Freedom is also the freedom not to choose. The law should not validate any category to which a citizen is supposed to belong – by nature, birth, culture or choice – which is not rescindable.

NOTES ON CHAPTER 6

1. Olivier Roy is a Researcher at CNRS, Paris, and is author of *The Failure of Political Islam* (Cambridge: Harvard University Press, 1994) and *Généalogie de l'islamisme* (Paris: Hachette, 1995).
2. See Emmanuel Todd, *Le destin des Immigrés* (Paris: Le Seuil, 1994).
3. Philip Lewis, *Islamic Britain* (London: I.B. Tauris, 1994), p 68.
4. See Kathleen Moore *Al Mughtaribun, American Law and the Transformation of Muslim Life in the USA* (New York: SUNY Press 1995), p 11: 'A key principle of this explicitly Islamic consciousness is that religious should prevail over ethnic identity'.

7

DEFINING NATIONAL IDENTITY IN A MULTICULTURAL SOCIETY

Bhikhu Parekh[1]

Every political community tends to, and needs to, form some general conception of the kind of community it is and would like to be, what it stands for, how it differs from others; in short, some view of its identity. National identity has nothing to do with national essence, spirit or soul, as Montesquieu and Herder argued, for no such thing exists, nor with what the nineteenth-century writers called national character or culture, for no modern society whose membership fluctuates and whose members take pride in self-determination can have a uniform character, and no modern culture is an undifferentiated and monolithic whole. National identity does not require collectively agreed national goals, for these are necessarily subject to dispute and constant redefinition, and it does not entail a uniform view of the country's history either, for its history is necessarily complex and contested, open to divergent narratives, and likely to prove deeply divisive if reduced to an exercise in national self-glorification.

Basically, the articulation of national identity has three components. The first of these is the constitution or the constitutive principles of a political community. The constitution represents the collective self-understanding of the community, the common platform on which its members have agreed to live together, and a clear public statement of its identity. No constitution is static, and formal and informal changes in it reflect and consolidate community members' self-understanding.

The second dimension of national identity has to do with the way a political community imagines itself. Political communities are highly complex entities, involving millions of people the individual member has never seen, but for whom he or she is expected to pay taxes, make sacrifices, and even die. They also encompass countless past and future generations, to whom each member is bound, again by common interests and attachments. Since the political community spans past, present and future generations and involves unseen millions, it requires a remarkable act of imagination, and is in that sense an imagined community, consisting in the way it is imagined, which includes both the style in which it is imagined and the content of that imagination.

Unlike the intellect, which is necessarily articulated and is only at home in the language of thoughts, imagination is necessarily articulated in the language of evocative images. Not surprisingly, images play a vital role in constituting and defining a community's self-understanding and identity. Indeed there is no community in history which has not sought to embody its collective identity in its self-image. Images crystallise and offer highly condensed and idealised accounts of what the community takes to be its ideals, values and organising principles, and represent its identity and distinctive contribution to the world. They are three-dimensional in nature, cognitive because they assert something about the community and are not fictitious in nature, effective because they arouse emotions, and conative because they inspire action. Since no community likes to think badly of itself, its dominant self-image is generally, though not always, benign.

Some examples will illustrate the point. The British tend to see their society as fair, decent, civil and committed to individual liberty. This self-understanding is neither wholly true nor completely false, and some evidence can be offered both for and against it. However, it reflects qualities the British like about themselves and wish to preserve. Since they define themselves in terms of these qualities, they seek to live up to them and feel or can be made to feel embarrassed and guilty when they do not. As they live up to their images of themselves, they become increasingly moulded to fit these images, and become what they would like to become. Images are not only self-projections, but also tools of self-creation.

What is true of Britain is true of other countries. The self-understanding of the United States is articulated through such images as liberty and equal opportunity, reflected in every American's alleged potential to move from the 'log-cabin to the White House'. Indians imagine theirs as a synthetic, tolerant and plural civilisation, and think that these qualities represent their unique contribution to the world. Mahatma Gandhi appealed to them to secure inter-communal harmony, and more recently many sensitive Hindus were deeply embarrassed, and even distressed, that some of the heirs of such a civilisation should have destroyed a mosque.

Images, then, are an integral part of national identity and a common currency of political and social discourse. Members of a community constantly invoke them to persuade each other to act in a particular manner, to support one policy rather than another, to follow one set of goals and not some other. Political discourse is not, and cannot be, exclusively argumentative or even deliberative, and contains an inescapable rhetorical element. The rationalists among us feel troubled by the fact that these 'irrational' elements play such an important part in political life, but this is a mistaken, even an irrational, response. Since much of the collective life is necessarily lived in imagination, it is only rational that it should be structured by somewhat vague but powerful images. Furthermore, the images have a cognitive content, and can and should be criticised, challenged and replaced over time by others. As they are revised, the community's identity undergoes a corresponding change. In collective, as in personal, life, self-understanding is articulated in, and derives emotional energy from self-images. We can criticise and revise them, but cannot dispense with them altogether. They constitute the community's cultural and emotional capital, and what they yield depends on how wisely they are defined and used.

The third component of national identity has to do with the way one relates to one's community. Identity is not a property, something we possess, but a relationship, a form of identification. National identity is about whether we identify with a community, see it as ours, are attached to it and feel bonded to our fellow-members in a way in which we are not bonded to outsiders. It implies that – however deep our disagreements and frustrations – we care enough for each other to want to continue to live together. Such commitment leads to mutual trust and goodwill, breeds a spirit of relaxed tolerance, and ensures that not every disagreement is feared as a source of subversion and secession. The commitment to the community clearly cannot be permanent and unconditional. I cannot be one of you if you refuse to accept and treat me as one, and I cannot be committed to you if you do not make a reciprocal commitment to me.

This shared sense of common belonging is embodied in and nurtured by such emotional symbols of collective identification as the national anthem, the flag, national ceremonies, rituals and monuments to dead heroes. These symbols play an important part in nurturing and vivifying national identity. They are symbols of our community, and not any other, and give it an unmistakable and tangible presence. They integrate us into the life of our community and link us to its past and future. They also mobilise political emotions, and give Habermas's highly cerebral notion of constitutional patriotism emotional and cultural depth. The symbols have the further advantage that they are largely formal and require no substantive commitment to a particular view of the country's history or collective goals. Once one has demonstrated one's commitment to the community by identifying with its cherished symbols, one has proved one's loyalty to it and need do no more.

National identity, then, is a matter of moral and emotional identification with a particular community based on a shared loyalty to its constitutive principles and participation in its collective self-understanding. It creates a sense of common belonging, provides a basis for collective identification, fosters common loyalties, and gives the members of the community the confidence to live with and even delight in their disagreements and cultural differences. If national identity in a multicultural society is to serve these purposes, it needs to satisfy certain basic conditions.

First, the identity of a political community is located in its political structure, and not in the widely shared personal characteristics of its individual members – in what they share publicly and collectively as a community, not in what is common to them as individuals. It should, therefore, be defined in politico-institutional rather than ethno-cultural terms, in terms of the institutions, values and mode of public discourse that its citizens can be expected to share as members of a community, rather than their psychological and cultural characteristics such as their habits, temperament, attitude to life, sexual practices, customs, family structure and hobbies. The ethno-cultural characteristics are too vague to specify and agree upon, are rarely shared by all or even a majority, pertain to their private lives, at best define a people and not a political community (Germans and French but not Germany or France), and can easily become an instrument for the suppression of unconventional life-styles and forms of behaviour.

Second, members of a multicultural society belong to different ethnic, religious and cultural groups, and these identities deeply matter to them. The prevailing view of national identity should allow for such multiple identities without subjecting those involved to charges of divided loyalties. There is no reason why one cannot be both Scottish and British, Quebecois and Canadian, Basque and Spanish, Breton and French, or Hindu or Sikh and British or French. Although there is in principle no conflict between ethnic, religious and other identities and the national one, it can arise if any of them were to be so defined as to exclude or undermine the other. If being British means being Christian or English, then clearly non-Christians and non-English cannot be British. And conversely if being Scottish were understood to involve being anti-English, or if being Muslim were to involve political loyalties and commitments incompatible with those to Britain and its political way of life, then these groups cannot be accommodated within even the most capacious definition of British national identity. If national identity is to leave sufficient space for other identities, both need to be defined in an open and inclusive manner and brought into at least a minimum level of harmony.

Third, the national identity of a community should be so defined that it includes all its citizens and makes it possible for them to identify with it. National identity is about who does or does not belong to the community and is or is not entitled to make claims on it. Minorities cannot feel part of a political community if its very self-definition excludes them and treats them as outsiders. When some leaders of the Malay community insist their country is Malay and not Malaysian Malaysia, they make the Malays the sole owners of the community and treat the Indians, the Chinese and others as outsiders who should be tolerated but not given equal rights and citizenship. When leaders of the Baltic Republics, Fiji, Trinidad, Guyana and other countries define their national identity in terms of the indigenous or numerically dominant community, their definition similarly excludes the minorities, be they Russians, Indians, Chinese, or erstwhile colonisers. Their usual defence is that the latter are recent arrivals, brought by the colonial powers, or planted by a dominant neighbour. The defence is flawed. Even many of the so-called 'indigenous people' can be shown to be outsiders if one goes further back in history, and differ from the rest in having arrived or been brought only a few decades earlier. Again, it is true that some of the minorities were recruited by colonial powers, but that is a legacy of history which cannot be undone and held against their present descendants, who have known no other home, struck their roots in the country, and identify with it. When individuals are born within or have lived long in a society and declare or demonstrate their willingness to remain its loyal members, their claims are just as strong as those who have lived for generations. This is why the term second or third generation 'immigrant' is deeply misleading. One might be the son or daughter of an immigrant but not an immigrant oneself, and one's ancestral origins cannot define one's current political identity or affect the quality of one's citizenship.

Finally, the definition of national identity should not only include all citizens, but also accept them as equally valued and legitimate members of the community. In many multicultural societies the majority community is willing to grant its citizens equal rights but feels possessive about the country, and insists that for democratic, historical and other reasons, the definition of national identity should reflect its centrality and enshrine its deepest cultural aspirations. While granting equal rights to all its citizens, the 1990 constitution of Croatia insists that it is the 'national state of the Croatian people' and realises their 'thousand-year dream' of an independent state of their 'own'. The constitution of Macedonia makes it the 'national state of the Macedonian people'. The Romanian constitution goes further. It gives equal rights to all its citizens but insists that the 'foundation of the state' is laid on the unity of the Romanian people, makes Romanian the official language of the country, makes 'Awake Romanians' the national anthem, and so on. In Malaysia three 'pillars' are considered central to its national identity, 'bahsa' (language, or Malay), 'agama' (religion, or Islam) and 'dan raja' (monarchy), all three closely connected with the majority. In Thailand, the three 'central elements' of national identity include 'sasana' (religion, or Buddhism), 'mahakasat' (monarchy) and 'chat' (nation), the first being the religion of the majority and the second the majority dynasty. Israel is officially a state of its Jewish majority, its name and all its national symbols are Jewish, its law of return privileges Jews, and so forth. Its Arab minority of just under 20 percent enjoys broadly equal rights with the rest, a secure cultural space of its own etc, but is barred, or 'exempted', from joining the armed forces and denied employment in enterprises associated with the military.

In all these cases the minorities feel aggrieved and alienated, and have often protested against their 'second-class' status. The Macedonian constitution, for example, was strongly opposed by and passed without the consent of its 30 percent Albanian minority. The Croatian constitution was criticised by its Serb, Slovene, Slovak, Hungarian and Muslim minorities. The Israeli, Malaysian, Thai and other definitions of national identity have provoked similar objections respectively from their Arab, non-Malay and non-Thai minorities.

The minorities contend that the state is officially appropriated by the majority community, and that they are treated as outsiders enjoying the status of protected minorities. They also argue that although they enjoy equal rights as individual citizens, they do not do so as communities for, unlike the majority community, they lack the collective rights of cultural and political self-expression and the opportunity to assert or acquire collective self-consciousness and a sense of collective agency. Minority communities insist that once the national identity is defined in a certain way, it generates popular pressure on the government to follow appropriate policies. Since Croatia, Macedonia and Romania are declared to be the national states of their dominant groups, these groups are seen as the authentic sons of the soil, more reliable and patriotic than the rest, more entitled to demand respect for their culture and religion, to be preferred over the rest in sensitive jobs, and so on. In Malaysia, for example, making Islam one of the three pillars of its national identity has encouraged many Malays to demand that it be declared an Islamic state, and has polarised the country between the Partain Islam, which supports that demand, and the United Malayas National Organisation, which opposes it.

Many of these and related minority criticisms are fully justified, and there is a strong case for defining national identity in a broad and collectively acceptable manner. By including minorities in the community's self-definition and giving them official recognition, such a definition legitimises and values their membership and can be accepted by them with enthusiasm. It protects the state against the kinds of nativist or majoritarian pressures mentioned earlier, and it does not undermine the inescapably dominant status of the majority, which is bound to assert itself in the normal political process anyway. Indeed, precisely because of this, it is in the interest of that majority not to 'rub it in' by enshrining its dominance too visibly and explicitly in the definition of national identity. When the majority organises itself and behaves as a nation and seeks to mould the state in its image, minorities too are led to define themselves as nations, or at least as ethnic groups. That polarises the political community and renders integration difficult. Both justice and political wisdom dictate that the majority community should resist the temptation to claim the cultural ownership of the political community.

Although this is the ideal to aim at, it is not always possible. The history of most countries is tied up with that of particular ethnic or cultural groups which have played a decisive role in their development, shaped their current character, and whose values and experiences are deeply inscribed in their major institutions: for example, the English in the UK, and the Anglo-Saxons in the USA. No society can negate its history and begin with a clean slate. Furthermore, some countries, such as Israel, have come into existence to realise the nationalist aspirations of the dominant communities, and cannot be expected to undergo radical changes, including name changes, anthems, self-definition etc, without alienating their majorities and suffering a profound moral disorientation and crisis of identity. Even when countries do manage to define their identity in non-communal terms, the influence of the majority community seeps through it in countless ways. India, for example, scrupulously resisted defining its national identity in Hindu terms, and yet its name ('India that is Bharat' as the very first article of its constitution defines the country), national anthem, national motto etc are all drawn from the majority Hindu tradition.

All this means that defining national identity in a multicultural society is an exceedingly difficult enterprise. It cannot, and should not be ethnically and culturally neutral, as it then satisfies nobody and lacks the power to evoke deep historical memories, but neither should it be biased towards a particular community as it then de-legitimises and alienates others, nor should it be culturally eclectic as it then lacks coherence and focus. There is no easy way to reconcile these and other conflicting requirements, and each political community has to strike its own balance. There are, however, several general considerations that could guide its choice.

Although a political community cannot deny or reject its historically inherited identity, it can officially declare itself multicultural, as Canada, Australia and other countries have done. This affirms its cultural plurality and counters such cultural biases as its self-definition, symbols and institutions contain. It is also sometimes possible to give the definition of national identity a broader meaning. Although Britain has traditionally been a Christian country, it is now religiously plural, and should be able both to define itself as multi-religious and find suitable institutional ways of expressing it. Prince Charles took an important step in that direction when he remarked that, as a monarch, he would like to be the 'Defender of Faith' rather than of 'the Faith', as is currently the case. Although well-meaning, even this does not go far enough, as it excludes those without faith or who do not think that their faith needs defence. A similar desire to multiculturalise national identity was at work when the newly independent state of India included the green colour of Islam in its national flag and Canada chose the maple leaf as a culturally impartial and nationally representative symbol of its identity.

Even when it is unable to avoid altogether the majority-based view of national identity, the political community can counter its symbolic and practical impact by providing ample autonomous cultural spaces to its minorities and making them a *de facto* part of its national identity. Although Buddhism is part of its national identity and figures prominently in its national rituals, the state of Thailand has allowed the Muslims of Southern Thailand to maintain their own religious schools and the 'khadi' courts to adjudicate matters relating to such things as marriage and the family. Israel's commitment to respect the Arabs' cultural identity, uphold their personal laws and fund their schools, and its requirement that all its citizens learn both its official languages, is another way of making national identity effectively plural. In the final analysis, the definition of national identity matters because it can de-legitimise minorities, damage their material and other interests, and make it difficult for them to identify with the political community. Once these are taken care of, it should not much matter if the definition of national identity retains some bias towards the dominant majority community.

NOTE ON CHAPTER 7

1 Bhikhu Parekh is Professor of Political Theory at the University of Hull. He is author of many works, including: *The Concept of Fundamentalism* (Leeds: Peepal Tree, 1992); *Gandhi*, Oxford: OUP, 1997); *Race Relations in Britain* (ed. with T. Blackstone and P. Sanders) (London: Routledge 1998).

PART IV

NATIONAL SELF-DETERMINATION

8

BEYOND THE FLAWED PRINCIPLE OF NATIONAL SELF-DETERMINATION

Adam Roberts[1]

In discourse on international relations, it is often assumed that the repeatedly-proclaimed right of self-determination means in practice a right of national self-determination. Yet there are grounds for doubt as to whether the right of peoples to self-determination, which is enshrined in international legal agreements, can, in general, mean a right to separate sovereign statehood. National self-determination can more usefully be viewed not as a legal right, but as a political principle – and a flawed one at that. It has often proved, in practice, disappointing and disruptive. A key question today is how international society is adapting, and moving beyond, this attractive but flawed principle; and what further steps in that direction might be taken.

The principle of national self-determination has by no means been wholly negative in twentieth-century history. Large imperial systems are inherently unstable, leading to strong pressure for self-rule in their constituent parts. At times when great empires have been threatened with defeat and collapse, the principle has been commonly advocated as a basis for a new and better order. The principle has helped to shape the responses of major powers to the break-up of empires, and it has provided a framework within which the attainment of national aspirations was assumed to encompass self-determination in the form of democratic institutions.

The proposition that political life should be based upon rational ordering principles, rather than upon an uncritical acceptance of existing arrangements and institutions, is part of our inheritance from the European Enlightenment. The application of this proposition to international relations – so full of tragic and violent clashes between rival kingdoms and empires – is entirely natural, and the idea of national self-determination has proved a key part of that application.

The central weaknesses of the principle of national self-determination are well-known. It has no authoritative exegesis. There has been a lack of clarity as to which 'peoples' or 'nations' are its bearers and supposed beneficiaries. Some of the most deplorable features of twentieth-century international politics – including the pursuit of irredentist claims and the cruel treatment of minorities – can in part be attributed to the principle and its defects. It has always been contested, and not only by the European colonial powers. At best it is only one principle among many, and needs to be balanced against other values and tempered by other considerations.

Nevertheless, ideas of self-determination in general, or national self-determination in particular, cannot be declared dead and then buried, with or without full military honours. They have shaped the world we inhabit, addressing central and enduring problems of international relations: the ways in which states are formed; the tendency of empires to decline and break up; the nature of post-imperial arrangements; the popular control of political power; and the vulnerability felt by peoples who do not have their own state. However, the flaws of national self-determination as an ordering principle are so numerous that there is a need to explore alternative bases of international order. The project of forming fully-fledged and sovereign nation-states – a project with which the principle is closely associated – needs to take its proper and modest place as only one of several ways of tackling the status of different communities in the international system.

MEANINGS OF 'NATIONAL SELF-DETERMINATION' AND 'NATION'

The principle of national self-determination, like all abstract political terms, has in the course of time undergone changes in meaning and connotation. However, its core meaning is relatively simple and uncontested. It is, as Cobban has put it, 'the belief that each nation has a right to constitute an independent state and determine its own government.'[2] It is generally associated with a teleological belief that when old empires are broken up into the more natural units of nation-states, there will be a better basis for democratic self-government within states, and peace between them. Although the term 'self-determination' is often used synonymously with 'national self-determination', it can also refer to other approaches to self-government, not so inextricably associated with the formation of independent states.

The core meaning of 'national self-determination' immediately raises the difficult question, what is a 'nation'? The term has a dual meaning: it can refer either to a people (even if not formed into a state), or to a state and all the inhabitants thereof. This duality is reflected in Cobban's definition of nation as 'a community that is, or wishes to be, a state'.[3]

In the first meaning, 'nation' can refer to a group of people who share a significant number (but seldom all) of such attributes as the following: history, language, ethnic origin, religion, political belief, fear of the same adversaries and a wish to live under political institutions which they can regard as their own. In this meaning, there is no assumption that the people concerned necessarily yet have a state. Nor need there be any assumption that they must in every case want to form one. Cobban himself, despite the words 'wishes to be' in his definition cited above, strongly opposes the idea that sovereign statehood is the only possible goal.[4]

In its second, and perhaps more popular, meaning, the word 'nation' refers to a political entity, namely an existing state or country, or simply to all the inhabitants thereof.[5] This meaning has triumphed in the very word 'international', and in the titles of major world organisations: the League of Nations, founded in 1919, and the United Nations, founded in 1945. Such usage of the term 'nation' to mean the same as 'state' is particularly common in the USA, and in the media more generally. It seems to imply, romantically but inaccurately, that every country is a 'nation' – a people with a sense of common identity. The term 'nation-state', often used as if all states were nations, conveys similar messages. The co-existence of these two distinct meanings of 'nation' has not assisted clear discussion of the principle of national self-determination.

WOODROW WILSON: FLAWED ADVOCATE

Two great exponents of national self-determination in the twentieth century have been V.I. Lenin and Woodrow Wilson. Despite the differences between them – not least in their views of democracy – both recognised the collapse of great empires as a central fact of their time; both saw the power of self-determination as a rallying-cry during and after the First World War; and both proved more willing in practice to ride rough-shod over the principle than their rhetoric might have suggested. Neither can be said to have developed a thorough and consistent theory about the place of self-determination in international politics.

The case of US President Woodrow Wilson is especially instructive. He is often seen as the leading visionary and advocate of the principle of national self-determination. His critics have sometimes accused him of blinkered idealism, and of conjuring up forces in Europe and beyond which he did not understand. Such views of his role in the years 1916–19 are too simplistic. True, in an important speech delivered almost a year before US entry into the war, announcing the USA's willingness to be a partner in an association of nations to secure basic principles of justice and peace, he spoke in idealistic terms: 'We believe these fundamental things: First, that every people has a right to choose the sovereignty under which they shall live...'[6] However, his policies were also hard-headed reactions to urgent practical problems: the inability of the Allied governments to agree on a clear set of war aims that would have public appeal; the desirability of enticing certain subject peoples to support the Allied cause; the need to cope with the collapse of the Russian, Austrian and Ottoman empires; and the requirement to respond to the strident advocacy of self-determination by Lenin and the Bolsheviks. He was attempting to bring some moral purpose and intellectual coherence to the US and allied responses to these problems.[7]

Wilson's speech of 8 January 1918, spelling out the Fourteen Points which he advanced as the essential terms for peace, is commonly cited as a high-water-mark of his advocacy of national self-determination. This conventional but mistaken view is reflected in a range of literature on the topic, and even in such mainstream sources as the *Encyclopaedia Britannica*:

> In his Fourteen Points – the essential terms for peace – US president Woodrow Wilson listed self-determination as an important objective for the postwar world; the result was the fragmentation of the old Austro-Hungarian and Ottoman empires and Russia's new Baltic territories into a number of new states.[8]

This passage, and others like it, is wrong about the content of the Fourteen Points speech and its relation to events. In his speech Wilson did refer to 'the preferences of the populations', and to 'the principle of justice to all peoples and nationalities'. However, he did not use the term 'self-determination' at all, and some of his proposals implied that other principles, including the maintenance of stability, loomed large in his mind. Like the other Allied leaders he was understandably reluctant to contemplate the collapse of the Austro-Hungarian empire.[9] This was the subject of his tenth point, which merely stated, 'The peoples of Austria-Hungary, whose place among the nations we wish to see safeguarded and assured, should be accorded the freest opportunity of autonomous development'. As for the Ottoman Empire, addressed in his twelfth point, he again used the phrase 'autonomous development' as a means of fudging the issue of the future of subject nationalities within the Turkish portions of the empire. All this was hardly a ringing endorsement of self-determination. However, one month after the appearance of the Fourteen Points, in another address to Congress, he did declare in general terms:

> National aspirations must be respected; peoples may now be dominated and governed only by their own consent. 'Self-determination' is not a mere phrase. It is an imperative principle of action, which statesmen will henceforth ignore at their peril... All the parties to this war must join in the settlement of every issue anywhere involved in it; because what we are seeking is a peace that we can all unite to guarantee and maintain and every item of it must be submitted to the common judgment whether it be right and fair, an act of justice, rather than a bargain between sovereigns.
>
> This war had its roots in the disregard of the rights of small nations and of nationalities which lacked the union and the force to make good their claim to determine their own allegiances and their own forms of political life. Covenants must now be entered into which will render such things impossible for the future; and those covenants must be backed by the united force of all the nations that love justice and are willing to maintain it at any cost.[10]

By October 1918, Wilson had been pressured by events to take the phrase 'self-determination' more seriously, and adopt a more radical position than he had in January on the future of Austria-Hungary. A message to the authorities in Vienna, even though it did not use the phrase 'self-determination', formally altered the tenth of his Fourteen Points:

> Since that sentence was written and uttered to the Congress of the United States the Government of the United States has recognised that a state of belligerency exists between the Czecho-Slovaks and the German and Austro-Hungarian Empires and that the Czecho-Slovak National Council is a *de facto* belligerent Government clothed with proper authority to direct the military and political affairs of the Czecho-Slovaks. It has also recognised in the fullest manner the justice of the nationalistic aspirations of the Jugo-Slavs for freedom.
>
> The President is, therefore, no longer at liberty to accept the mere 'autonomy' of these peoples as a basis for peace, but is obliged

> to insist that they, and not he, shall be the judges of what action on the part of the Austro-Hungarian Government will satisfy their aspirations and their conception of their rights and destiny as members of the family of nations.[11]

Wilson's application of the principle of self-determination to key problems was thus a response to events in Europe as much as it was their cause. Yet there were legitimate fears that his advocacy of self-determination would have major and adverse political repercussions. His own Secretary of State, Robert Lansing, warned on 30 December 1918:

> The more I think about the President's declaration as to the right of 'self-determination', the more convinced I am of the danger of putting such ideas into the minds of certain races. It is bound to be the basis of impossible demands on the Peace Congress and create trouble in many lands... The phrase is simply loaded with dynamite. It will raise hopes which can never be realised. It will, I fear, cost thousands of lives.[12]

Lansing was right to fear dynamite, but it existed anyway, at least in Europe, in the form of powerful competing nationalist movements. Perhaps the more valid part of his criticism of Wilson is that, faced with the growth of nationalist movements and numerous claims to statehood, the great prophet of self-determination was vague. Along with other statesmen of his time, he failed to make clear in public statements what was recognised well enough in the actual conduct of negotiations: that any right of self-determination could only be applied very unevenly, and with due regard to circumstances and to other principles. Frequently, indeed, Wilson betrayed the very principle he proclaimed, and did so without explanation.[13] His defenders do not provide convincing answers to such charges.[14] He tended to retreat into vacuous generalisation, as his own account of a meeting with a group of Azeris in Paris in 1919 suggests:

> Do you know where Azerbaijan is? Well, one day there came in a very dignified and interesting group of gentlemen who were from Azerbaijan. I didn't have time until they were gone to find out where they came from. But I did find this out immediately – that I was talking to men who talked the same language that I did in respect of ideas, in respect of conceptions of liberty, in respect of conceptions of right and justice.[15]

Wilson was not alone in being uninformed about the different peoples and regions with which he had to deal. Harold Nicolson, a member of the British delegation at the Paris Peace Conference, writing a letter to his wife Vita, complained about meetings between Prime Minister David Lloyd George, French leader Georges Clemenceau and President Wilson:

> But, darling, it is appalling, those three ignorant and irresponsible men cutting Asia Minor to bits as if they were dividing a cake... Isn't it terrible – the happiness of millions being decided in that way – while for the last two months we were praying and begging the Council to give us time to work out a scheme?[16]

WEAKNESSES OF THE PRINCIPLE OF 'NATIONAL SELF-DETERMINATION'

Although it remains a very uncertain guide to dividing the cake, the principle of national self-determination has been associated with the most important revolution of the past 50 years: the process of European decolonisation and the consequent emergence of new or reconstituted states. It contributed to the view that white racial domination is, or at least ought to be, a thing of the past. After 1989, it provided one basis for the emergence of new states from the ruins of the Soviet Union and the former Socialist Federal Republic of Yugoslavia. It helped to legitimise the single most important change of European borders since 1945, namely the unification of Germany in 1990. There is plenty of life left in this old principle.

Yet all too often the principle of national self-determination seems to be part of the problem, not part of the solution. The central weakness of the principle is that it appears to assume that each specific 'people', or 'nation', is neatly arranged on the map, and only awaits liberation from outside control in order to assume its rightful place in a peaceful and democratic international order. The vision is attractive, seductive and misleading. It has run into trouble twice in Europe: first in the period after the First World War, and second in the 1990s. It is worth examining more closely some of the problems which have arisen in practice both in Europe and elsewhere.

Which Peoples are Appropriate Candidates for Self-determination?

Perhaps the most difficult practical question arising in all the attempts to apply the principle of national self-determination in the twentieth century has been deciding which units are appropriate candidates for self-determination. This question can be put more simply as: Who is the 'self' in 'self-determination'?

The deliberations and outcomes of the 1919 Paris Peace Conference illustrate not only the difficulty of the question, but also the ways in which disputes about it can lead to new wars.

It came to be widely felt, at least in the areas concerned, that the general principle of national self-determination had not been applied at all, or had not been applied properly, to: German minorities in various countries; Hungarians left outside the reduced borders of Hungary; the inhabitants of many European colonies; and the Kurds in various countries of the Middle East. This outcome of the Paris Peace Conference arose because the rights of one nation had to be balanced against those of others, and the very principle of national self-determination had to be balanced against other principles and interests, including respect for the rights of many existing states and empires. The result was that the Paris Peace Conference was perceived as basing the international system on a principle which was not fairly implemented: this was a prime cause of the system's declining legitimacy and ultimately of war.

In the United Nations era, resolutions of the UN General Assembly (and, to a lesser extent, the Security Council) have sometimes contained more or less authoritative determinations of what constitutes an appropriate candidate for self-determination. Such resolutions have also provided one basis for states to refuse to recognise certain situations which involved a denial of self-determination. Rhodesia's unilateral declaration of independence on 11 November 1965 was opposed by the UN, and more generally by the international community, partly because the continuation of white minority rule was manifestly not a case of self-determination.[17] Yet in general the UN's record in identifying candidates for self-determination is one of limited success, mainly because the task itself is so inherently problematic.

Problems of deciding on the appropriate units of self-determination sometimes arise not only where a people is denied sovereign statehood, but also in cases where a people is divided into several states. The huge 'Arab nation', encompassing as it does a large number of states, is a notable case in point. Although pan-Arabism has lost some of its force, and there is very little advocacy of a vast Arab union, the idea that there is an Arab nation highlights the artificial character of many of the territorial divisions within the Arab world. It also compounds the complexity of determining who the 'self' is in self-determination.

The most common problem arising from the uncertainty about the units entitled to self-determination concerns secession. For a long time, the principle of national self-determination was advocated in the context of the break-up of formal empires, especially the European overseas empires. But there is no reason why it should stop there. The principle of self-determination can also be espoused by national groups within a state. Many contemporary conflicts are between post-colonial governments and minorities demanding self-determination. Distinct peoples within a new state, to which they may feel little allegiance, often seek to secede and set up their own separate state. Following European decolonisation, only a few such secessionist movements have managed to create new states: Singapore, Bangladesh and Eritrea are leading examples. There is a strong presumption against secession. African governments have been opposed to changes in their post-colonial arrangement of states and frontiers, however artificial these may be, because they understandably fear that permitting secession would set a destabilising precedent.

There have been countless cases in which distinct geographical areas, containing a people who certainly have some common interests and fears, have not been considered appropriate candidates for self-determination. Two conspicuous examples under British rule have been the Falkland Islands and Hong Kong. In both cases it has been widely felt that asserting a right of self-determination would make matters worse with the major power claiming sovereignty over the territory. Thus, in the dispute with Argentina over the Falklands, the British have consistently undertaken to respect the 'interests' of the inhabitants of the Falklands, but have refrained from promising to observe their 'wishes', which would involve an implied right of self-determination.

A special difficulty has arisen concerning the possible application of the principle of national self-determination to indigenous peoples. In many countries, for example in Latin America and Australasia, there are one or more indigenous peoples who see their position as that of the colonised. The governments of the countries they inhabit are deeply reluctant to view them as possible candidates for self-determination. In discussions among representatives of indigenous peoples held under UN auspices, there have inevitably been proposals to assert a right of indigenous peoples to self-determination, which could easily be seen as implying national self-determination. These proposals have caused considerable controversy. There is the risk that they could encourage false hopes, and lead to dangerous confrontations. They have also led to an attempt to redefine self-determination in this context, that is to point it away from claims to full statehood.[18]

The understandable reluctance of states to see the principle of national self-determination universally applied has led to successive attempts to tame the doctrine by limiting its scope. In the twentieth century there have at various times been implicit or explicit assumptions that the principle of national self-determination only applied to: empires defeated in war (eg Habsburg, Ottoman); former European colonies, separated from the metropolitan power by salt water; Israeli-occupied territories and South Africa; collapsed communist federations in a manifest state of turmoil.

There has also been an implicit doctrine – which emerged under communist rule in the Soviet Union and the Socialist Federal Republic of Yugoslavia, and has also been evident in the post-colonial world – that the exercise of a right of self-determination was something which only occurred once, at a specific historical moment. If a free choice had supposedly been made by, say, Croatia, to form part of the Yugoslav federation, that decision was final. Like a Catholic marriage, freely entered into, it was a decision made for life. Sometimes a more general extension of this doctrine could be detected: peoples which had failed to secure independent statehood at an earlier historical period had somehow 'missed the historical bus', and could not expect another one to turn up.

Difficulty of Determining Where Boundaries Should Lie

Even when a people has been accepted as having a right of self-determination, the question of how the boundaries of its state should be defined has proved perennially difficult. One answer frequently given has been the holding of plebiscites, through which the inhabitants of a given area can decide whether or not they wish to form part of one or another state. However, this answer is not as simple as it sounds. Someone, and usually some power, has to decide in what area such a plebiscite should be held, and what question should be asked. This often comes close to a decision on where the boundary line should run. The question of whether, and where, to hold such plebiscites is extremely controversial.

The principle of self-determination is commonly said to lead to the danger of 'balkanisation'. It has indeed been a major contributory factor in the process of 'fission' of larger units into smaller ones which has been such a notable feature of international politics in the post-1945 period – not in principle a negative development. However, balkanisation implies not just the creation of small states, but also the continuation of conflict. In many parts of the Balkans, instability has often arisen from the fact that drawing boundaries on the basis of nationality is well-nigh impossible: any imaginable set of borders gives rise to irredentist claims and provokes conflict.

Partly because of fears such as these, outside powers negotiating settlements based on self-determination have often tried to create larger units than a strict application of the principle might seem to require. They did so at the 1919 Paris Peace Conference, creating the huge and apparently artificial Kingdom of the Serbs, Croats and Slovenes (which from 1930 called itself Yugoslavia). The creation of Czechoslovakia (which in its original form contained many ethnic minorities) was a similar case. It was not only external powers which preferred to create a few large states rather than many smaller ones. Local political forces and leaders often had their own agendas, involving distressingly imperial elements. Power politics is by no means the exclusive preserve of the great powers.

Small national entities have often had doubts about whether they can survive and flourish within lines drawn on the map on the basis of ethnicity. Thus there are often pressures to expand their borders to include economic assets, key elements of transport networks, and strategically defensible frontier areas. Czechoslovakia, the post-1919 nation-state which had the best prospect of defence against Nazi Germany, had its defences mainly in the Sudetenland, a largely German-inhabited area which was lost at Munich in 1938 partly because of the strength of the appeal of national self-determination, both locally and in international diplomacy.

Because devising new state boundaries on the basis of ethnic or any other principles is notoriously difficult, the essentially conservative idea has developed that any new state emerging from an old empire should accept the old colonial or administrative frontiers. Not only did most European decolonisation follow this approach, but a new version of it emerged in response to the collapse of the Soviet Union and Yugoslavia from 1991 onwards. A dubious doctrine was espoused that if a federal state collapses, then its existing component parts – if they determine through democratic means that they want independence and also make appropriate commitments to uphold human rights – should be recognised as the legal successors. A central difficulty of this approach was that the internal borders of these two great federal socialist states, the Soviet Union and Yugoslavia, did not always follow clear ethnic or other defensible lines. Some of the emerging states contained large and dissatisfied minorities.

There appears to be no escape from the dilemmas which have produced these conservative doctrines regarding frontiers. Governments around the world remain unwilling to take self-determination to its logical conclusion, whereby people can 'self-determine' in what state they should live and where its boundaries should run.

Failure of New States to Remain Democratic

In much advocacy, national self-determination was coupled with democracy, and with the creation of a new order in which all citizens could have a full participatory role in the affairs of their state. As Cobban put it, 'By 1918 nationalism and democracy were generally taken as synonymous in the thought of the Western nations'.[19] The reality has all too often been different. Many new states established in the name of national self-determination have not remained democratic for long, and have engaged in oppressive treatment of minorities.

Eastern Europe in the 1920s and 1930s is a case in point. Hopes that there would be a new democratic order after 1919 were quickly dashed. Within some of the new states, especially Yugoslavia, political parties were formed on an ethnic basis and assumed a conflictual character. Many of the crises of democracy were made worse by difficult external circumstances. Economic problems in the new states, leading for example to hyperinflation in Hungary, were exacerbated by the effects of the depression. By the late 1930s, only Czechoslovakia remained democratic.

Comparable problems arose in many post-colonial states from the 1960s onwards. Hopes that decolonisation would lead to a new democratic order were often disappointed. This was partly because of a flaw at the heart of the theory of national self-determination. In most countries, it is not self-evident that the 'nation' is all the inhabitants: it may merely be a dominant group, or indeed an elite claiming to represent that group. The doctrine can easily lead to the oppression of minorities by the dominant majority. Indeed, in some newly-independent successor states there may be several groups which all see themselves as oppressed 'nations', or at least demand certain distinct national rights.

One central difficulty of the application of national self-determination has always been the problem of minorities. This question arose in 1848, in relations between revolutionary Hungary and its many Serb subjects. Like leaders of many a newly-emerging nation in more recent times, the Hungarian leaders were unwilling to grant to their Serb and other minorities anything approximating to those national rights they claimed for themselves.[20] It was the tragedy of the Hungarian revolution of 1848–9, and of much of the history of the Magyar people, that the contribution to the emancipation of other nationalities in the region was so negative.[21]

Perhaps the worst aspect of the principle of national self-determination is the idea, from which it cannot easily be separated, that the state is the manifestation of what might be called an 'ethnos' – a particular ethnic group. Such an idea can only too easily lead to intolerance of other groups in society, even to ethnic cleansing as a cruel way of making reality conform with theoretical prescriptions.[22]

Some governments and political movements have developed anti-democratic perversions of the idea of national self-determination which can be called 'national determinism'. One form is the idea that all individuals are born with an ethnic identity which cannot be varied by any act of will: whatever their actual wishes, or subjective sense of identity, destiny dictates that they are part of a given nation; they must, in a sense, be forced to be free. There is not much self-determination in this idea. The second, related, form of national determinism is based on the proposition that a given territory should be united, irrespective of the wishes of the actual current inhabitants. Such a view has at times informed the actions of the various factions of the Irish Republican Army, which has sought the unity of the island of Ireland despite the fact that a majority of those in the North (and probably also a majority in Ireland as a whole) do not want it. China's claims to Taiwan also have overtones of such 'national determinism'. The implicit endorsement by the UN General Assembly of such principles of justice as the retrocession of colonial enclaves also contains more than a hint of national determinism, and may in some instances have encouraged certain decisions to resort to force.

Potential for Internal and International Instability

The disjunction between 'nation' and 'state' has been a central cause of the great majority of wars and civil wars of the twentieth century, including two world wars and most wars of the post-1945 era. The principle of national self-determination has the merit of addressing this cause of war, but it can also have the effect of making it worse. It can provide a series of justifications for uses of force, and it can, paradoxically, help to create the circumstances in which war may break out.

The achievement of self-determination by India in 1947 is a case in point. Much of the confrontation between Indian nationalists and Britain in the four decades up to 1947 was relatively peaceful, yet the consequences of the decision to quit were violent. It was not obvious what the successor units to the British Raj should be. The decision to create the separate Muslim state of Pakistan was followed by the huge death toll in the Hindu-Muslim riots around the time of independence, and by continuing tensions between India and Pakistan, including several inter-state wars, one of which (in 1971) resulted in the creation of Bangladesh.

If a significant proportion of the inhabitants of a region of one state want their region to be transferred to another state (or are merely suspected of so wishing), then armed conflict within that region, and sometimes even war between the two states concerned, becomes a strong possibility. Hence the difficulties over Kashmir since 1947, the events leading to the Turkish military intervention in northern Cyprus in 1974, and the conflict in Northern Ireland from 1968 onwards.

Such problems are not surprising. The achievement of self-determination often leads to the emergence of a new entity whose constitutional system, regime, and frontiers lack legitimacy. It is no accident that the great majority of UN peacekeeping operations since 1945 have been in relation to post-colonial conflicts.

The problems faced in former Yugoslavia and the former Soviet Union were even more difficult than those encountered in European decolonisation in the years after 1945, a slower, and sometimes a more controlled, process, in some cases made easier by the distance between the metropolitan country and the colonies. It is not surprising that they caused a series of wars with a strong international dimension.

Czechoslovakia is the main exception to the generalisation that the break-up of former socialist federal states leads to conflict. The bifurcation of Czechoslovakia on 1 January 1993 was achieved without outbreaks of violence either before or after the event. There are two main reasons for the peaceful character of this process: first, the country had over centuries developed an unusually non-violent political culture, and second, the existing frontier marked a broadly acceptable line between the Czech Republic and Slovakia.

Three Disruptive Aspects of Struggles for Statehood

The struggle of a nation seeking to attain statehood poses special and potentially disruptive problems. Three which have proved perennially difficult are: what political leader or entity represents the nation? What means of struggle should be pursued? May outside powers give support to national liberation movements?

If determining which peoples are appropriate candidates for self-determination (discussed earlier) poses problems, so does the question of who represents a nation before it has attained independent statehood. There have been many tragic episodes, including several at Paris in 1919, in which unofficial representatives of subject peoples were simply ignored by the statesmen of the time, storing up resentment and hostility for the future. Sometimes outside powers have supported different national liberation movements within a country, thus contributing to civil war there: this happened in Angola during and after Portuguese rule, leading to a disastrous war which has endured from Portugal's withdrawal in 1975 right up to the present day. Sometimes, too, there is deep rivalry between bodies based outside the territory (for example, governments in exile), and leaders operating inside.

One possible way of resolving these problems is for international organisations (whether regional or global) to decide that a particular body is (in the language used by the UN General Assembly in respect of the PLO and SWAPO) 'the sole legitimate representative' of the people concerned. This can assist in a resolution of the issue, but it involves risks: the body concerned, basking in the glow of international approval, can easily get out of touch with opinion within the territory, or become intransigent in its dealings with adversaries; and other organisations, resenting the discrimination against them, may seek allies among local powers. One normal means of resolving such disputes – the holding of elections – is usually not available in the territories concerned.

A second disruptive issue concerns the methods of struggle which may be pursued in trying to achieve statehood. The recognition of self-determination as an international right has reinforced (though it certainly did not create) the tendency of national liberation movements to view war as a legitimate means of pursuing their just aims; and it has also reinforced the tendency of interested outside powers to lend support to such struggles. In all the UN General Assembly debates touching on this matter, two issues have been largely obscured from view. First, there has been practically no discussion of the possibility that in some instances the cause of national liberation may be more effectively pursued by peaceful means, ranging from diplomatic pressure to non-violent struggle in the territory itself. Second, very little has been said about the applicability of the laws of war to combat by national liberation movements or other insurgents, a matter tackled separately, and with limited practical effect, in the 1977 Geneva Protocols I and II, additional to the four 1949 Geneva Conventions.

A third disruptive issue concerns what kind of assistance struggles for national self-determination may receive from outside. The UN General Assembly's attempt at legitimation of such assistance (eg in the 1970 Declaration on Friendly Relations, discussed further below) actually provides a possible basis for confrontation and conflict. Equally, both the Soviet doctrine of national liberation and the Reagan doctrine as it developed in the early 1980s provided a strong political justification for military support within other states in cases where that support was deemed to be assisting the cause of self-determination.

IS 'NATIONAL SELF-DETERMINATION' RECOGNISED IN INTERNATIONAL LAW?

The post-1945 period has seen a historically unique emphasis on the principle of self-determination. International legal agreements concluded under UN and other auspices refer to it extensively, but do not specifically mention national self-determination, whose legal status is at best ambiguous.

The *UN Charter*, Article 1(2), refers to 'equal rights and self-determination of peoples'. This phrase was unclear both about what a 'people' was and about whether self-determination required separate statehood for each people. It was deliberately used in the charter because it was imprecise. To the governments which drew up the charter it was more acceptable than the worryingly precise and heavily encrusted term 'national self-determination', which was uncomfortably definite about the rights of all nations to form sovereign states, and which was seen as having played a fateful role in the instability and conflict in Europe in the inter-war years.

In the decades after 1945, as the UN's membership grew to encompass post-colonial states, self-determination came to be increasingly emphasised, and given a more specific meaning. A number of UN General Assembly resolutions enshrined the idea of self-determination, often in language which came close to a right of national self-determination, but for the most part in the context of advocating the end of 'colonial' rule. An early example of this approach was the 1960 *Declaration on the Granting of Independence to Colonial Countries and Peoples*.[23]

In October 1970, the General Assembly adopted a *Declaration on Principles of International Law concerning Friendly Relations and Co-operation among States in Accordance with the Charter of the United Nations*. This offered two potentially contradictory principles touching on the question of self-determination. On the one hand it approved: 'The principle that States shall refrain in their international relations from the threat or use of force against the territorial integrity or political independence of any State...'

This involved respect for sovereignty, and might be taken to imply that states could not threaten or use force even against a state that was denying self-determination to all or part of its own people. On the other hand, principle (e) on 'equal rights and self-determination of peoples' seemed to negate the above-mentioned rule. In its subsequent elaboration of this principle the document actually went so far as to say:

> Every State has the duty to refrain from any forcible action which deprives peoples... of their right to self-determination and freedom and independence. In their actions against, and resistance to, such forcible action... such peoples are entitled to seek and to receive support in accordance with the purposes and principles of the Charter.[24]

Similar tensions between the inviolability of sovereignty and the right to support liberation struggles arose in the Declaration of the 1993 World Conference on Human Rights in Vienna.

The right of self-determination has also found reflection in a number of formally binding legal agreements. Article 1, paragraph 1 of the *International Covenant on Civil and Political Rights*, adopted in 1966, states: 'All peoples have the right of self-determination. By virtue of that right they freely determine their political status and freely pursue their economic, social and cultural development.' Identical wording appears in the parallel *International Covenant on Economic, Social, and Cultural Rights*.

Another major treaty, the 1977 *Geneva Protocol I*, not only recognises self-determination as a legitimate goal, but also embodies a degree of legal justification for the use of force in attainment of that goal. Article 1(4) states that the Conventions and Protocol apply in:

> armed conflicts in which peoples are fighting against colonial domination and alien occupation and against racist régimes in the exercise of their right of self-determination, as enshrined in the Charter of the United Nations and the Declaration on Principles of International Law concerning Friendly Relations and Co-operation among States in Accordance with the Charter of the United Nations.

Thus 'self-determination' has been repeatedly proclaimed in authoritative political and international legal documents as a right of 'peoples'. Such pronouncements have led some to conclude that self-determination is a legal right which actually means in effect national self-determination;[25] but much legal analysis has been cautious, especially on account of the difficulty of determining which peoples are the bearers of this right and whether statehood must be their destination.[26]

In the many pronouncements and debates in a UN framework, such delicate questions as who the appropriate candidates for self-determination are, and whether secession from existing states can be permitted, have for the most part been neglected. However, there has been a tendency to imply that self-determination only pertains to peoples under colonial domination, alien occupation (e.g. the Israeli-occupied territories) and racist regimes (eg South Africa during the *apartheid* years). It is difficult to limit the application of broad principles in this way, and inevitably leaders of many other peoples, in justification of their particular cause, have referred to the various general UN pronouncements on self-determination. To the extent that the UN has become associated with ideas of national self-determination, it may have contributed to the growth of some conflicts as well as the resolution of others. However, it has stopped just short of upholding a general right of national self-determination.

THE LIMITS OF NATIONAL SELF-DETERMINATION IN THE 1990S

Despite all the advocacy of self-determination in a UN framework, there is evidence of growing recognition that the principle, at least when it means national self-determination, is dangerous in its practical implications. A significant sign of a shift away from general advocacy of national self-determination came from UN Secretary-General Boutros Boutros Ghali in his 1992 report *An Agenda for Peace*:

> The United Nations has not closed its door. Yet if every ethnic, religious or linguistic group claimed statehood, there would be no limit to fragmentation, and peace, security and well-being for all would become ever more difficult to achieve.[27]

The claims of many peoples to self-determination are still greeted mainly by an embarrassed silence from the international community: the cases of Chechnya, Tibet and East Timor illustrate the point. 'National self-determination' remains powerful as a battle-cry for political and military action, but it has not been advocated in the 1990s as a theory for international order, or as a possible path to international peace. The movements towards self-determination in the 1990s have taken place without the dubious benefit of any high-profile general advocacy of the idea by leading statesmen. Wilsonianism seems as dead as Leninism.

The Break-up of Yugoslavia and the Soviet Union

When the Socialist Federal Republic of Yugoslavia and the Soviet Union broke up, the principle of national self-determination made a positive contribution by assisting the creation, quite largely by consensus, of successor states. However, there was also a negative role. In many cases, peoples were not arranged on the map in a way which enabled them to form states, and many bitter wars with an ethnic dimension resulted, as for example between Armenia and Azerbaijan, and between Serbia and Croatia. In particular, within some of the successor entities, claims to national rights by minorities (for example, the Serbs in Croatia and Bosnia) contributed to the outbreak of wars. No less bitter were the conflicts resulting from the claims to statehood of peoples within larger federations, as in the cases of Chechnya and Kosovo.

In its response to the break-up of these two great socialist federations, the international community was, as always, torn between conflicting principles of self-determination on the one hand, and preservation of order on the other. In the summer of 1991, as both Yugoslavia and the Soviet Union were disintegrating, the United States resisted the logic of collapse and opposed self-determination for longer than was prudent – just as it had been reluctant to contemplate the collapse of the Habsburg Empire three-quarters of a century earlier. In the end, a residual acceptance of self-determination, tempered by scepticism and by pressure for proper consideration of minorities, did influence the behaviour of the international community (including the USA) in response to the collapse of the Soviet Union and Yugoslavia.

Germany seems to have been motivated more than other states by a belief in national self-determination, but its resulting policies on Yugoslavia were acutely controversial. It forced the pace of European Community recognition of Croatia, which took effect on 15 January 1992, even before Croatia had met EC conditions for minority protection. This action, which exacerbated the tragic problem in Bosnia-Herzegovina, was the outcome of a feeling that Germany had recently benefited from national self-determination, and could not therefore deny the principle to others. There does not appear to have been much awareness at the time of the sheer difficulty of applying the principle of self-determination to the complex ethnic realities of former Yugoslavia, especially Bosnia, the problems of which were not well understood in Germany or indeed in the rest of Western Europe. This experience, and especially the failure to stop the wars in Bosnia and Croatia, added to the scepticism in Western Europe about the adequacy of national self-determination as a basis for order.[28]

The Post-colonial Order

A key remaining question is the extent to which the post-colonial order, especially in Africa, is now under threat, and the ways in which this exposes weaknesses in the idea of national self-determination. By the early 1990s the old post-colonial order was showing more signs than ever of cracking at the seams. Somalia's descent into chaos in 1992 was partly a consequence of its artificiality as a state, and its loss of superpower support once the Cold War was over. Successor entities, including Somaliland, have emerged in parts of the country, but are unrecognised. In Ethiopia, Eritrea finally succeeded in breaking away in 1993 after a long war and a UN-monitored referendum – the first major post-colonial secession since that of Bangladesh in 1971–4. Such cases show that to achieve independence it is often still necessary to fight for it. From 1994 onwards, the crises in Rwanda and Burundi showed how tragically flawed was the 'self-determination' of the post-colonial order.

The question of what are the appropriate units of self-determination remains difficult in several instances. For example, in the cases of Western Sahara and East Timor, there are strong arguments for self-determination, but the states which seized these territories militarily in 1975 and remain currently in charge (Morocco and Indonesia respectively) are reluctant to concede that they are appropriate units for statehood, and argue that these territories have never had any continuous existence as internationally recognised sovereign states.

East Asia

The question of national self-determination arises in many forms in East Asia. Korea is a relatively simple case in theory, even though turning theory into practice will be even harder than usual. Both North and South support the cause of unification. The fact that they at present have different ideas of how it should be achieved, and what the political system of a unified Korea should be, may not be a permanent obstacle – especially as the regime in the North, not being particularly successful either at building communism or at unifying the country, will not last for ever. However, the experience of Germany's absorption of East Germany (a far easier task by comparison) has contributed to extreme caution about the character, pace and direction of unification of the two Koreas. It is as if national unification could be safely advocated when it seemed unattainable, but is treated with more caution once it begins to look possible. The federal or confederal arrangements that are being considered for Korea are the only ways of approaching this issue.

China presents some of the most serious and complex challenges of national self-determination. Put at its simplest, the question has long been, and remains, whether the proper unit of self-determination is 'greater China', including for example Tibet and Taiwan, or whether these territories themselves constitute proper units of self-determination.

The situation of Hong Kong is technically the simplest, so far as the question of national self-determination is concerned. Remarkably, although Hong Kong is one of the most flourishing and successful city-states in the contemporary world, virtually no-one has considered it a possible candidate for national self-determination. The sense of Chinese identity of its inhabitants, the fact that the New Territories were incorporated into Hong Kong by a 99-year lease signed in 1898, the territorial contiguity with China, and the vast preponderance of Chinese power have all militated against self-determination. The negotiations leading to the 1984 Sino-British Joint Declaration, ratified in 1985, centred on securing recognition for a measure of autonomy for the Hong Kong Special Administrative Region of the People's Republic of China, commencing on 1 July 1997. Thus history, especially in the form of ancient treaties, shapes current options. Critical issues regarding post-1997 Hong Kong include maintenance of an honest and impartial civil service, a respected and independent judiciary, honest competition in banking and business, and a free press. All this requires enough of a change in China's mind-set and administrative practices without raising the issue of national self-determination.

The argument about Tibet's status is largely about its history. Those who support its right to independence assert that before its incorporation into the People's Republic of China, Tibet had a high degree of independence and autonomy. Insofar as it accepted suzerainty arrangements, they were not exclusively with China. The facts of Chinese power, and the Chinese reluctance to admit criticism and to change course, militate strongly against achieving a major change of policy in the near future. Recognising this, the exiled Dalai Lama, in various proclamations in recent years, has called for an arrangement with the People's Republic of China that would not necessarily involve complete Tibetan sovereignty, but his modest proposals have not been accepted by the Chinese Government.

Taiwan similarly illustrates the importance of history, but has achieved more success in asserting a separate status. Taiwan certainly has a distinct identity, forged by its history, including the interactions of Japanese, Chinese and US influences. For much of the nineteenth century, China – with its conception of a universal state system in which aborigines were to be brought in gradually and voluntarily – exercised partial control over Taiwan.[29] China can only be said to have been fully recognised as controlling the whole island for a very short period: from 1874 until 1895, when Taiwan fell under Japanese control.[30]

The claim that independence should be Taiwan's goal, not unification with China, thus has some historical basis. Proponents of this view assert that a right to self-determination means a right to separate existence as an independent sovereign state. Taiwan's abortive move in the 1990s for admission to the United Nations was destined to fail. Nonetheless, the case for maintaining Taiwan's independent identity has continued to resonate internationally because of two factors. First, China's military pressure on Taiwan has forced many countries, including the USA, to reiterate their strong opposition to the use of force over the issue. Second, Taiwan's move towards a much more democratic political system has struck chords with the USA and other countries. It is impressive that in the presidential election of 23 March 1996 some 75 percent of Taiwan's voters supported candidates who favoured open or tacit independence.

Against claims for Taiwanese independence lies the argument that it is not so long since the Taiwanese authorities themselves argued that China was one country (and they were the legitimate representatives of all of it). More important is the harsh fact that Beijing is consistently and bitterly hostile to all efforts to exclude any territories from a reuniting China. The lack of flexibility in Beijing is compounded by the fact that the regime's principal justification for maintaining its monopoly on power is essentially more national than communist: its historic mission, and a large part of its *raison d'être*, is to create a proud and independent China that can stand on its own feet. It seeks to complete that struggle against economic backwardness, military weakness and subjection to colonial indignity on which the Chinese Communist Party embarked in the years after its formation in 1921.

Thus the question of Taiwan might seem to be a classic case of a theoretically unresolvable conflict between independence on the one hand and incorporation into China on the other. Some have sought a way out of this conflict by seeing Taiwan as having a potential role in reforming China. As one writer has put it, Taiwan 'might be able to gradually democratise communist China', and its role in shaping China's 'direction, its behaviour, its politics and its defence priorities could be critical'.[31] Yet there is not much sign that China will acquiesce in policies aimed at subverting its political system. An alternative approach could try to develop the idea of a Chinese commonwealth: taking the principle of 'one country, two systems' further, in the direction of recognising a variety of different statuses and administrative systems within an overarching concept of one China. This implies accepting an ambiguity about the status of Taiwan which takes us away from distinctively modern (and some would say Western) ideas of statehood.

The experience of the 1990s in East Asia and elsewhere seems to confirm a curious and paradoxical truth: a principle that was conceived as a way of providing for self-determination, implying a choice by individuals in determining the very shape of the state in which they live, has come to be reinterpreted in what might unkindly be called a reactionary way. This reinterpretation implies a right to statehood in cases where there is some previous history of independent existence as a state; or where a political entity has had previous existence as a distinct unit within a federation. The international community's emphasis on the desirability of referenda (as in the former Yugoslav republics) does involve a genuine element of determination by the 'self', but only in circumscribed ways. Any other approach, according complete self-determination and rights to form a state to any group wanting it, is too open-ended and disruptive. We all seem to be caught in a web of history in this way: self-determination seems to yield to a kind of historical determinism.

BEYOND TRADITIONAL CONCEPTIONS OF SELF-DETERMINATION

The principle of national self-determination, though long advocated as a basic norm of international relations, might wither on the vine. Following its own successes, the principle might lose its relevance as peoples come to accept the existing order of things. This is what has in fact happened in large parts of the world, including post-colonial areas. States have a mutual interest in accepting their existing frontiers, irrespective of their dubious origins and weak ethnic logic. Their inhabitants, too, generally prefer an anomalous status quo to the uncertainties of trying to change it.

Yet such a comfortable and conservative approach is of little help with the hard cases, and it is in those cases that the principle of national self-determination is most likely to be invoked. Self-determination still lives as a powerful political presence partly because of the sheer strength of nationalism in the contemporary world. As Anthony Smith has written:

> despite the capacity of nationalists to generate widespread conflict and destruction, the nation and nationalism provide the necessary socio-cultural framework for a modern politically plural order. They have no real rivals in the contemporary world.[32]

National self-determination also flourishes because it is far from obvious what other principle can be invoked to try to explain and justify the present arrangement of the world into 185-plus sovereign states of such radically differing shapes, sizes and national histories. The idea that there is a right to national self-determination has not been exhausted by the process of European decolonisation. It acquires a special force when peoples feel their existence or identity threatened. Where there is extreme oppression, and a reasonable prospect of establishing a new state, the case for going down the path of national self-determination is still strong.

However, there should be no illusions that this principle can always be applied, and on a basis of consensus. The theory of national self-determination was sometimes conceived of as providing a means of eliminating one of the major causes of war; but only on rare occasions has it been implemented without war. Some peoples have emerged to statehood on the basis of a remarkable degree of unanimity among their immediate neighbours and the major powers: Namibia and united Germany are recent examples. In many other cases, national self-determination has only been accepted when it has been fought for. Woodrow Wilson's reluctance to call for the destruction of the Habsburg Empire during the final year of the First World War, at least until local forces had fought for their right to independent existence, had echoes in the cautious US policies towards the former Soviet Union and Yugoslavia at the end of the Cold War.

Because of its many failures, the lesson of experience in the twentieth century is that the idea of national self-determination needs to change, and to be supplemented by other ideas.[33] As Antonio Cassese has put it in the concluding words of his thoughtful survey of self-determination, there is a need 'to rethink even the most fundamental, seemingly axiomatic, premises of that central concept – self-determination – which has overshadowed so much of this century'.[34] The following three propositions point to some obvious possible directions.

First, self-determination should be distinguished from national self-determination and become a more open-ended concept. Self-determination can reasonably be interpreted not in terms of one single end-result, namely sovereign statehood, but in terms of process.[35] It can imply a commitment to democracy, or to negotiation towards a special political status, within existing larger political frameworks. This view was taken emphatically by the Supreme Court of Canada in its 1998 landmark decision in the case of *Certain Questions Relating to the Secession of Quebec from Canada*.[36]

In UN debates and studies in the 1990s there has been a tendency to free the idea of self-determination from its earlier association with the idea of sovereignty, and to view it much more as an entitlement to democracy. In a 1995 study of minority problems conducted under UN auspices, Asbjørn Eide, Director of the Norwegian Institute of Human Rights, reached conclusions highly critical of national self-determination, but favourable towards a modest interpretation of self-determination as a more open-ended concept:

> The controversies over alleged rights to self-determination by groups living within sovereign states have severely obstructed peaceful solutions of contemporary ethnic conflicts. It is therefore recommended that the Sub-Commission [on Prevention of Discrimination and Protection of Minorities] study the meaning and scope of self-determination for groups living within sovereign states.[37]

It is not necessarily a matter of going back in time to the traditional attempt to devise safeguards under the heading of 'minority rights'. Some minority problems can be most usefully addressed simply as general constitutional or human rights issues, an approach which has the merit of not labelling one group as constituting a problem and receiving special benefits. Ideas and practices of consociationalism also have a part to play.

Second, states need to be seen as more than merely the embodiment of a single 'nation'. In the theory of national self-determination, the state is often seen as the embodiment of one particular group, namely the 'nation', and this group is often understood in ethnic terms. Such a view, while it has great strength, especially in threatened communities, needs to be supplemented or even supplanted. There are many other visions of the role and character of states: as an administrative unit responsible for specific areas of territory and all the inhabitants thereof; as an instrument for mediating conflicts between its citizens, including group conflicts between different peoples or regions; as a mini-alliance of more or less independent entities; and as a mechanism for safeguarding certain legal, administrative, cultural or religious standards, including international human rights standards.

In any given case, even a partial redefinition of the nature and function of states along the above lines has to be managed with extreme delicacy. It does not necessarily involve either weakening the state or abandoning all aspects of a state's self-understanding. In post-Cold-War Europe, human rights and national minority questions have become a matter of international interest and involvement, including through bodies such as the Council of Europe and the Organisation for Security and Co-operation in Europe. Their approach to such questions has generally been one of accepting the continued role of strong states, regarding human rights norms as equally applicable to all states, and trying to get questions resolved without resort to such devices as the minority rights treaties imposed on certain relatively weak states after the First World War. This approach, involving modest redefinitions of the functions of states, has had some successes.[38]

Third, there should be more open acceptance of the possibility of variations, ambiguities and anomalies in the status of many territories. Although in theory the world of the late twentieth century is one of equal sovereign states, some ambiguities and anomalies in the status of certain territories remain; and there may be a need for more flexibility about the status of territories if many difficult contemporary problems are to be addressed effectively.

An acceptance of irregularities might seem to go against the grain of the contemporary world. The UN Charter, Article 2(1), enshrines the principle of 'the sovereign equality of all its Members'. The commitment of international organisations in the UN period to the global application of this principle is historically unparalleled. The decolonisation process has powerfully reinforced the view that full sovereign statehood is the most basic institution of the contemporary international system.

By contrast, almost all earlier systems of states contained strong elements of suzerainty and other types of formal or informal relationships of dominance.[39] Many such elements have remained features of international relations in the UN era, sometimes concealed behind the appearance of full statehood, sometimes more overt.

Without entering into that huge body of international relations literature on whether the role of the state may now be declining, it is clear that the contemporary world is characterised by different levels of authority (local, regional and global) for different purposes. The idea of the completely independent sovereign state is tempered by the practical need to respond to strong local identities; and also to co-operate internationally in a wide range of activities, which often means setting up authorities with some elements of supranationalism. These complex and multi-layered arrangements of the contemporary world have echoes of the Middle Ages in Europe.

Arrangements involving anything approximating to suzerainty are not likely to be openly accepted as legitimate core components of the contemporary international system. However, some aspects of such arrangements, especially the underlying idea that some territories and peoples need a special status short of full sovereign statehood, have a useful role today, and will continue to do so throughout the twenty-first century. There is a need to recognise this fact more openly, and to consider the possibilities of various types of special status in addressing contemporary problems. From Kosovo to Korea, Kurdistan to Hong Kong, Transylvania to Taiwan, there are elements of, and a continuing need for, special arrangements which modify the concept of a separate national existence that has been the goal of movements for national self-determination.

Possible forms which such arrangements can take include autonomy, international administration, joint sovereignty, federations and confederations within a state, and commonwealths encompassing distinct entities. Such arrangements may be permanent or temporary – though in international relations, temporary arrangements sometimes last for a long time. They have disadvantages. They often seem to be a 'second best' for sovereign statehood: the latter was preferred by many of the peoples for whom Wilson proposed autonomy in January 1918. They can give outside states a legitimate interest in 'internal' matters of a country, thus providing a possible basis for certain uses of military force. They pose problems regarding membership of such entities in international organisations. Their record is mixed.[40] Yet they are consistent with some ideas of self-determination, and offer a more fruitful way of thinking about certain international problems than does the still-living, but all too limited, principle of national self-determination.

NOTES ON CHAPTER 8

1 Adam Roberts is Montague Professor of International Relations at the University of Oxford, and a Fellow of Balliol College. He is the author of many works, including *Nations in Arms*, 2nd ed. (London: Macmillan, 1986) and *Humanitarian Action in War*, IISS Adelphi Paper no. 305 (Oxford: Oxford University Press, 1996). He is grateful to Erica Benner, Paul Chen, Mary-Jane Fox and Andrew Hurrell for their suggestions and comments on earlier drafts.

2 Alfred Cobban, *The Nation State and National Self-Determination*, rev. ed. (London: Collins Fontana Library, 1969), p 39.

3 *Ibid.*, p 108.

4 *Ibid.*, eg at pp 129 and 149.

5 As late as 1878, the Dictionary of the Académie Française still gave as the primary definition of the nation 'the totality of persons born in a country and living under a single government'. Here the nation is apparently seen as the reflection of a political entity – ie state or country.

6 Woodrow Wilson, address at a banquet of the League to Enforce Peace, 27 May 1916: *Congressional Record*, vol. 53, part 9, p 8854.

7 For a succinct and critical view of Woodrow Wilson's international leadership in the context of the events of 1917–19, see Arthur S. Link, *American Epoch: A History of the United States Since the 1890s* (New York: Alfred A. Knopf, 1955), pp 218–31.

8 Article on 'self-determination' in the *New Encyclopaedia Britannica*, 15th ed., 1989, Micropaedia, vol. 10, p 619.

9 The Fourteen Points, contained in Address of the President of the United States Delivered at a Joint Session of the Two Houses of Congress, 8 January 1918: *Papers Relating to the Foreign Relations of the United States*, 1918, Supplement 1, The World War (Washington DC: US Government Printing Office, 1933), vol. 1, pp 12–15.
10 President Wilson, Address at a Joint Session of the Two Houses of Congress, 11 February 1918, *ibid.*, 1918, pp 110–11.
11 Robert Lansing, Secretary of State, to the Swedish Minister (Ekengren), 19 October 1918, for transmittal to the Austro-Hungarian Government. Text in *ibid.*, p 368.
12 Robert Lansing, *The Peace Negotiations: A Personal Narrative* (London: Constable, 1921), p 87.
13 For details of the numerous departures from self-determination in the Paris negotiations at the end of the First World War, see Lansing, *The Peace Negotiations*, *op. cit.*, pp 85–7. On Wilson's vagueness about the conduct of negotiations, see ch. xvi, 'Lack of an American Programme', pp 169–89.
14 For a stout defence of Woodrow Wilson's role in the Paris negotiations, and of his advocacy of self-determination, see Ray Stannard Baker, *Woodrow Wilson and World Settlement: Written from his Unpublished and Personal Material* (New York: Doubleday, 3 vols., 1922), vol. 1, pp 11–22.
15 Woodrow Wilson, Luncheon Address in San Francisco, 18 September 1919: Text in Arthur S. Link (ed.), *The Papers of Woodrow Wilson* (Princeton: Princeton University Press, 1990), vol. 63, p 348. See also the similar remarks eight days earlier: *ibid.*, p 157.
16 Harold to Vita, Paris, 4 May 1919: text in Nigel Nicolson (ed.), *Vita and Harold: The Letters of Vita Sackville-West and Harold Nicolson* (London: Weidenfeld & Nicolson, 1992), p 83.
17 James Crawford, *The Creation of States in International Law* (Oxford: Oxford University Press, 1979), pp 104-6.
18 See Christian Tomuschat (ed.), *Modern Law of Self-Determination* (Dordrecht: Martinus Nijhoff, 1993), esp. Gudmundur Alfredsson, 'The Right of Self-Determination and Indigenous Peoples' and Douglas Sanders, 'Self-Determination and Indigenous Peoples'.
19 Cobban, *The Nation State and National Self-Determination*, *op. cit.*, p 43.
20 R.W. Seton-Watson, *The Southern Slav Question and the Habsburg Monarchy* (London: Constable, 1911) pp 46–7.
21 A theme stressed in Robert A. Kann, *The Multinational Empire: Nationalism and National Reform in the Habsburg Monarchy 1848-1918*, vol. 1, *Empire and Nationalities* (New York: Columbia University Press, 1950), pp 123–4.
22 The practice of 'ethnic cleansing' is of long standing. Theories of national self-determination did not create it, but may have made the practice worse in the twentieth century. For a succinct survey, see Andrew Bell-Fialkoff, 'A Brief History of Ethnic Cleansing', *Foreign Affairs*, New York, vol. 72, no. 3 (Summer 1993), pp 110–21.

23 Annexed to GA Res. 1514 (XV) of 14 December 1960. On the basis of this declaration, the General Assembly established a 'Special Committee on the Situation with regard to the Implementation of the Declaration on the Granting of Independence to Colonial Countries and Peoples'.

24 Annexed to GA Res. 2625 (XXV) of 24 Oct. 1970.

25 For a measured exposition of the view that the right of self-determination has acquired a true legal status in the UN era, largely due to the sheer political pressure stemming from the decolonisation process, see A. Rigo Sureda, *The Evolution of the Right of Self-Determination: A Study of United Nations Practice* (Leiden: Sijthoff, 1973), esp. at pp 26–7 and 3526.

26 For judicious and critical evaluations, including of UN documents and debates, see Muhammad Aziz Shukri, *The Concept of Self-Determination in the United Nations* (Damascus: Al Jadidah Press, 1965); Michla Pomerance, *Self-Determination in Law and Practice: The New Doctrine in the United Nations* (The Hague: Nijhoff, 1982); Antonio Cassese, *Self-Determination of Peoples: A Legal Reappraisal* (Cambridge: Cambridge University Press, 1995).

27 Boutros Boutros-Ghali, *An Agenda for Peace* (New York: United Nations, 1992), para. 17.

28 For a critical evaluation of the European Community and US record on self-determination with respect to Yugoslavia, and of the work of the Badinter Commission, see Kamal S. Shehadi, *Ethnic Self-Determination and the Break-up of States*, Adelphi Paper 283 (London: Brassey's for International Institute for Strategic Studies, 1993), pp 28–31.

29 Sophia Su-fei Yen, *Taiwan in China's Foreign Relations, 1836–1874* (Hamden, CT: Shoe String Press, 1965), pp 290–1.

30 Some even put the starting date for full Chinese control later, in 1887, when the island was made a province. See eg Laura Tyson, 'Strained Relations in Family Feud', *Financial Times*, London, 2 June 1995, p 13.

31 Gary Klintworth, *New Taiwan, New China: Taiwan's Changing Role in the Asia-Pacific Region* (Melbourne: Longman; New York: St Martin's Press, 1995), pp 242, 243.

32 Anthony Smith, 'Ties That Bind', *LSE Magazine*, London, vol. 5, no. 1 (Spring 1993), p 11.

33 Contemporary attitudes to self-determination, including reconsideration of several aspects, are usefully presented in Donald Clark and Robert Williamson (eds), *Self-Determination: International Perspectives* (London: Macmillan, 1996).

34 Cassese, *Self-Determination of Peoples: A Legal Reappraisal*, *op. cit.*, p 365.

35 For a rich discussion of this issue, see Benedict Kingsbury, 'Claims by Non-State Groups in International Law', *Cornell International Law Journal*, vol. 25, no. 3 (1992), esp. at pp 486–8 and 500–3.

36 Richard G. Dearden, 'Can the Government of Quebec Break up Canada Unilaterally Under International Law?', *International Law*

News, Section of International Law and Practice, American Bar Association, Washington DC, vol. 28, no. 1 (Winter 1999), pp 15, 16, 23.

37 Asbjørn Eide, *Peaceful and Constructive Resolution of Situations Involving Minorities* (Oslo: Norwegian Institute of Human Rights, 1995), p 155. See also his chapter 'In Search of Constructive Alternatives to Secession', in Tomuschat (ed.), *Modern Law of Self-Determination*, *op. cit.*, pp 139–76.

38 For a succinct survey of these developments in Europe from 1990 onwards, see Jennifer Jackson Preece, *National Minorities and the European Nation-States System* (Oxford: Clarendon Press, 1998), pp 123–77.

39 Adam Watson, *The Evolution of International Society: A Comparative Historical Analysis* (London: Routledge, 1992).

40 For a useful and succinct survey of autonomy arrangements around the world, see Ruth Lapidoth, 'Autonomy: Potential and Limitations', *International Journal on Group Rights* (Dordrecht), vol. 1 (1994), pp 269–90. For a fuller study, see the same author's *Autonomy: Flexible Solutions to Ethnic Conflicts* (Washington, DC: US Institute of Peace Press, 1997).

9

THE RIGHT OF SELF-DETERMINATION

Danilo Türk[1]

GENERAL REFLECTIONS

Everybody will agree that the issues of self-determination are politically sensitive and that consequently a great deal of caution is required in dealing with the abstract concepts pertaining to self-determination.

A recent UN experience can be mentioned as one among many illustrations. In 1993, the General Assembly discussed the proposal made by Liechtenstein to study the realisation of self-determination through the principle of autonomy. The basic idea of that proposal, namely to explore the possibilities of using 'autonomy' to address issues of self-determination, and at the same time to preserve the territorial integrity of existing states, seemed promising. However, in a political context such as that of the UN, the fear of unwanted political consequences prevailed over an idea which appealed to common sense. Hence, the General Assembly decided at the same session in 1993 to defer further discussion of the Liechtenstein proposal *sine die*. This example illustrates one among the many difficulties of dealing with self-determination, that raised in addressing its abstract and potentially disruptive aspects. Notwithstanding its inconvenient character, however, self-determination remains politically relevant, and therefore has to be on the international agenda.

Since 1991, the emergence of a number of new states in Europe and the former Soviet Union, and the resulting issues of their recognition and admission to international organisations, represented one of the important items on the international agenda. Self-determination was relevant to these issues in some cases as a means of legitimation of the claims for independent statehood, and in some other as a means of *ex post facto* explanation of the emergence of new states. In the UN, the issue of non-self-governing territories continues to be a subject of discussion. There are, at present, 17 such territories. The General Assembly resolutions generally reaffirm the relevance of self-determination in this context and recommend different methods to ascertain the wishes of the populations concerned. In some cases, the UN recognises the need to use the method of referenda to enable the people concerned to express its will. In some difficult cases before the UN, like those of Western Sahara or East Timor, the UN and other international bodies have not been successful in their attempts to find solutions. Furthermore, it is necessary to keep in mind that a number of other situations in which claims for self-determination have been put remain outside the reach of the UN or any other organised international process. Sometimes these situations continue to be characterised for protracted historical periods by political and military conflict.

It is not surprising that in view of such diversity no coherent and internationally accepted political doctrine of self-determination exists. The enunciation of the principle of self-determination – in such international instruments as the two *International Covenants on Human Rights or the Declaration of Principles of International Law on Friendly Relations and Co-operation among States*, in accordance with the Charter of the United Nations (1970) – has not so far yielded a coherent body of interpretation and application. Thus the emphasis put by the Human Rights Committee (an expert body established to supervise the implementation of the *International Covenant on Civil and Political Rights*) on internal self-determination and democratic governance – an important aspect of self-determination – cannot be interpreted to mean that internal self-determination represents the right or, perhaps, even the only answer in all circumstances. In matters related to external self-determination, the practice of states seems to have been motivated mainly by political considerations and by the exigencies of each situation, rather than by a need to develop a coherent and predictable body of practice which would help in the interpretation and application of the principle of self-determination as a principle of international law in the future situations.

A general observation can be made that the principle of self-determination is being historically reaffirmed as a powerful mobilising principle. On the other hand, it has not been applied in all relevant situations, and has not been always used as a guiding principle to the political decision-makers. Political selectivity remains an important feature here. Furthermore, the principle of self-determination has been less than reliable as an organising principle. It has not yet been developed to a level at which it would enable the definition of appropriate legal regimes for different situations. At the level of its current legal formulation it remains open-ended and imprecise. As a part of international law it addresses, as French jurist Alain Pellet remarked, categories such as 'the people', 'free will' and 'freely chosen political status' rather than definitions, and in addition it does not define with precision the duties of states corresponding to the right of peoples.[2] For these reasons it seems necessary to enquire whether one can detect elements of criteria for the application of the principle of self-determination in the history of its practical realisation.

THE RIGHT OF SELF-DETERMINATION IN HISTORICAL PERSPECTIVE

The need for identification of criteria for the application of the principle of self-determination clearly exists and it can be approached in a variety of ways. Before trying to suggest elements of a general approach, I wish to explore two basic elements of self-determination, namely the people claiming self-determination and the political status which is the object of their claim. I believe that it is useful to explore these key notions in a historical context; in particular, it is necessary to mention three historical situations of self-determination: first, the collapse of the Austro-Hungarian, Ottoman and Russian empires; second, the process of decolonisation; third, the dissolution of the three socialist federations in Europe (Soviet Union, Yugoslavia and Czechoslovakia).

I am not suggesting that we enter into an in-depth historical discussion, but rather that we identify the importance of what can be learnt from these situations for the two central notions of self-determination, the people and the political status claimed.

The final stage of the dissolution of the three great multinational empires took place during World War I and in the ensuing new territorial and political arrangements formulated at the Peace Conference starting in 1919. That period was characterised by Lenin's and Wilson's insistence on self-determination as an essential organising principle of the post-World-War-I world.

The holders of the right of self-determination were ethnically defined peoples ('ethno-nations' in the modern sociological terminology). The new maps had to be drawn without a solid basis of prior political arrangements or boundaries. The principle of *uti possidetis*, used in Latin America and later in Africa, was not, and probably could not be, applied in the post-World-War-I Europe.[3] The political status granted to the peoples concerned was that of independent statehood. The approach taken was not, and probably could not be, applied consistently, and large minorities existed in the new states. In the cases of Poland and Romania, for example, about one third of their populations were persons belonging to minorities. In the case of Czechoslovakia and the Kingdom of Serbs, Croats and Slovenes (later called Yugoslavia) a fundamental contradiction existed in the very structures of the state. Neither of the two had a single ethnic majority, something of paramount importance in nation-states, but both were unitary states and resembled nation-states in their legal outlooks.

The issue of national minorities was very serious in those circumstances. The Nazi manipulation of the German minorities in Czechoslovakia and Poland contributed significantly to the outbreak of the World War II, and to the expulsion (or 'transfer' in the terminology of the post-World-War II arrangements) of German minorities from central European states at the end of that war. The ethnic structure of some central European states became simpler, and the issue of minorities was de-internationalised for an extended period of time (until the 1990s). The issue of self-determination was, with the exception of the division and later re-unification of Germany, temporarily removed from the European agenda. The peoples in the three socialist multinational federations seemed to be satisfied with the type of self-determination provided within the Soviet Union, Czechoslovakia and Yugoslavia. Their claims re-emerged only after the collapse of socialist systems in Europe.

Before addressing the issues resulting from that collapse, it is necessary to make a few remarks on self-determination in the context of decolonisation. This is necessary not only because of the temporal sequence of events, but also for conceptual reasons related to the key notions of 'the people' and the 'claimed political status'.

From today's perspective, decolonisation seems to have been historically inevitable and relatively uncontroversial. It is perceived as a clear and legitimate case of self-determination and, according to some commentators, a process which has exhausted the use of self-determination provided for in the international legal instruments of our time. The paradox here lies in the tendency of commentators to characterise the historically preceding case of self-determination as the final one. Thus Winston Churchill, in a statement in the House of Commons in 1943, emphasised that the reference to self-determination in the Atlantic Charter related to the need to defeat Nazi domination over the peoples in Europe, and had no relevance to the colonies. In a similar manner, many commentators during the immediate post-decolonisation period characterised self-determination as an essentially anti-colonial principle inapplicable elsewhere.

From the standpoint of the two basic questions concerning the notions of 'the people' and the 'claimed political status', the arrangements resulting from decolonisation were relatively clear and looked simple. The holders of the right were peoples, understood not as ethno-nations but as populations of entire colonial territories. The frontiers of these territories remained generally unchanged, in accordance with the principle of *uti possidetis*. The political status obtained was independent statehood for these territories, which now became sovereign states. As a result, the membership of the United Nations tripled in its first three decades, something seen at the time as an achievement and sign of the organisation's vitality. The fact that populations of entire colonial territories were accepted as holders of self-determination was a matter of historical necessity. Any other arrangement was likely to create more difficulties. However, it would be wrong to conclude that the post-colonial arrangements were ideal or 'superior' to the post-World War I model. They were simply different because they were dictated by different circumstances.

The subsequent experiences have varied. Although on the whole the post-colonial arrangements were viable, there were also such experiences as the partition of India and the dissolution of Pakistan, as well as, on the other side of the spectrum, the territorial expansion of Indonesia. The need to develop the many former colonial territories into nations in a political sense remains important, and the processes of nation-building are fraught with dangers – as experienced in Congo and Nigeria and more recently in Uganda, Rwanda and Burundi. Even Somalia, which was perceived as relatively homogenous ethnically, has undergone collapse. Whether Zaire (since 1997 the Democratic Republic of the Congo) will be able to continue to exist as a single state is unclear.

The post-colonial experience has influenced the entire body of thinking about self-determination. The extreme example of that influence was the view that decolonisation exhausted the meaning of self-determination. That view was proven untenable by the dissolution of the three multinational socialist federations in Europe – the Soviet Union, Yugoslavia and Czechoslovakia. Three specific features characterised these situations.

The first was that of ethnic complexity. Yugoslavia never had a single ethnic majority, while in Soviet Union and Czechoslovakia political balance among the main ethnic groups was necessary for the larger systems to work. The second was ideological and constitutional. All the three federations were created on the Lenin's conceptualisation of self-determination. The principal federal units (the republics) were constituted in a manner which gave the populations of those republics the status of 'peoples', and therefore holders of the right of self-determination. The republics resembled nation-states, created on the basis of ethnic principle, but they were not defined in ethnic terms only. Socialism was supposed to be a system of political and social relations which would gradually develop a conflict-free society in which the ethnic element was expected to become irrelevant. This was a utopia, of course, yet a powerful one: it was pursued for a number of years, and it worked to some extent. The third specific feature was the constitutional recognition in all the three federations of the right of separation of each of the republics from the rest of the federation.

The three socialist federations provided new answers to the two basic questions of self-determination, namely what constitutes the people and what political status that people is entitled to. The peoples were the populations of the socialist republics which had an ethnic core but were, as political communities, defined not only in ethnic terms. The political status of these peoples was defined by the status of the republics within the federation, and the possibility of change towards independent statehood was one of the aspects of that political status. The idea of the right of self-determination as a continuously existing right was expressed in the respective constitutions. When these three federations dissolved, they were succeeded by the former republics, which became sovereign successor states.

The collapse of socialism as an ideology and a socio-political system created the circumstances in which the three socialist federations ceased to exist. Each of them had a different fate which need not be discussed in this context. It is important to say, however, that without the larger process of change which entirely transformed the social and political landscape of Central and Eastern Europe, the collapse of the three socialist federations would not have occurred, and consequently the status of independent statehood would not have become an option for the peoples of the socialist republics constituting the three federations. In this last of the three historical situations mentioned here, as in that of the dissolution of the multinational empires after the First World War and that of decolonisation after the Second World War, the time and circumstances in which the right of self-determination was realised were not, and could not be, sufficiently predictable to make the identification of specific criteria of self-determination possible.

SUGGESTIONS CONCERNING THE CRITERIA FOR SELF-DETERMINATION

In assessing the legitimacy and realism of a claim for self-determination, or lack thereof, it is necessary to carefully consider all the relevant facts of the situation at hand. But can a policy-maker facing a specific situation benefit from a set of specific criteria agreed to by states, or at least having broad support in the doctrine of international law? A short and somewhat simplified answer would be that the practice of states does not follow a coherent pattern which would allow for a positive answer. However, there exist convincing arguments supporting the idea of legitimacy of self-determination in certain circumstances. Three such types of argument can be quoted:

One argument is the liberal one based on the idea that a people ought to have the right to 'opt out' from the larger system because the contrary view would inevitably justify oppression. Legitimacy of any government must be based upon the consent of the governed, and the governed will be in control of their destiny only if they have the right to withdraw their consent. In cases where the notions of 'the governed' and 'the people' coincide, the people always has the right to the appropriate form of self-determination.

The liberal argument is logical yet not necessarily practical. It leaves open questions which necessarily require a degree of co-operation (eg the identification of boundaries and the fate of minorities) and which may, if left unaddressed, create conflict which would otherwise not have occurred. Furthermore, it does not propose criteria for identification of the distinctiveness of a people from another people – a problem which can be quite considerable in circumstances not characterised by a violent conflict. Neither does it help where there is a need to choose among different statuses of self-determination. The practical problems in the application of the liberal argument are such that it is not likely that it would help commentators or decision-makers in formulating their position when faced with a politically complicated, yet non-violent, situation in another country. It is likely that in such circumstances the argument of non-interference in domestic affairs of another state will prevail over the liberal argument in favour of self-determination. In the case of a violent conflict which identifies the people with some clarity and makes the political options definable, the holders of the liberal view would probably support the claim for self-determination at an early stage.

In view of the difficulties of the liberal approach, other approaches have been advanced. According to some commentators the main criterion should be the right of peoples to self-preservation and defence against discrimination, massive violations of their human rights and genocide. When confronted with the threat to, or even outright attack on, their existence, peoples have the right to opt out.

This approach is less coherent, because it tries to bring under a single roof a variety of different situations. In cases of discrimination or violations of human rights, the problems are essentially the same as those characterising the liberal approach. Why should anybody outside the country concerned advocate self-determination as a remedy for discrimination or violation of human rights? Wouldn't it be natural to strive for more specific remedies, and at the same time preserve the territorial integrity of the country concerned? It seems that certain forms of self-determination, including territorially-based autonomy, can be combined with specific remedies to redress discrimination or eliminate human rights violation. Genocide and other threats to the very existence of the people are accepted by many commentators as valid reasons to accept claims for self-determination. Many would agree that in those situations in which the facts of a genocide became proven beyond doubt, self-determination, most probably in the form of independent statehood, is the only answer. However, it does not seem satisfactory to wait until the situation deteriorates to such a stage. It would be far more satisfactory if self-determination could be applied in a manner preventing genocide. This would require an assessment of political facts and a judgement of whether they constitute a genuine threat to the existence of a people. As in the case of the application of the liberal argument discussed earlier, it would seem likely that the concern for the preservation of the territorial integrity of states will prevail over the preventive application of the right of self-determination.

The preceding two arguments for self-determination are based on such concepts as legitimacy, human rights and the right of peoples to exist. Another approach which I would call 'the argument of a comprehensive political calculation' introduces additional political criteria for self-determination, such as the representativeness of the government and the degree of destabilisation caused by self-determination.

According to this argument, explained recently by Professor Frederic Kirgis, the international acceptability of a claim of self-determination depends on a combination of the degree of destabilisation resulting from the claim,[4] and of the degree of representativeness of the government affected by the claim. Generally, the claims which are more destabilising (for example, a bid for secession) are less likely to be recognised, even if the affected government is not representative. Conversely, less destabilising claims, like those aiming at (greater) autonomy within a state, are more likely to be accepted even if the affected government is fairly representative. However, if a government is quite unrepresentative, the international community may recognise even a seriously destabilising self-determination claim as legitimate. The application of these criteria of representativeness and destabilisation requires an assessment of the specific circumstances of a situation at hand and a margin of discretion in the analysis of the relevant facts. The opinions on the degree of representativeness of a government, and of the actual destabilising potential of a claim for self-determination, are necessarily subjective. Therefore, the conceptual soundness of this approach may not guarantee the desired level of its practical usefulness.

An additional criterion which might help in assessing actual situations lies in the principle of 'effectiveness' which belongs to the essentials of international law. There are two ways in which this criterion can be, and sometimes actually is, used. It is used in determining whether sovereign statehood, the object of most claims for self-determination, has been achieved or has the prospect of being achieved. The recognition of new states and rejection of unrealistic claims are the two basic types of outcome of the application of the principle of effectiveness in such circumstances. A second way of applying the principle of effectiveness becomes relevant when the international community wishes to support an obviously legitimate claim of a group trying to realise self-determination within parameters defined by the criteria of representativeness and destabilisation. If such a group does not effectively control the territory, then the international community might consider offering it political support, including its recognition as an emerging state, as well as other practical assistance. Obviously, the risk here is that an incorrect assessment and an unduly activist approach may result, in violation of the principle of non-intervention in the internal affairs of an existing state. On the other hand, an unduly timid approach might stimulate the use of force against self-determination, with resulting unnecessary suffering.

These three arguments concerning the application of the principle of self-determination – the liberal argument, the right of self-preservation argument, and the effectiveness argument – can be used individually or in combination. A discussion on their use would probably show that none of them is entirely satisfactory as a tool to help decision-makers assess a specific situation and suggest appropriate action. A certain level of subjective political judgement will continue to be necessary.

IN CONCLUSION

Developments in the last few years have once again confirmed the power of self-determination as a mobilising and primarily political principle. Although claims for independent statehood come in waves, and there are long periods when the most dramatic aspects of self-determination do not occur, it has to be assumed that self-determination will continue to pose important and difficult questions to the international community. Legal instruments and judicial and quasi-judicial bodies such as the Human Rights Committee will continue to have only a limited role in matters of self-determination. International political bodies such as the UN Security Council and General Assembly will probably continue to grapple with some of the issues of self-determination, but they may not include the most important ones. Furthermore, international institutions act upon an agreement among governments, and usually arrive late. The burden of assessment of situations, and of decision-making, will therefore continue to be carried by governments individually.

It is certainly necessary that certain objective criteria are developed to assist governments in their assessment and decision-making. While an abstract formulation of these criteria, such as the one offered in this presentation, is not likely to be satisfactory, the general parameters which can be deduced from international norms and practices will help.

NOTES ON CHAPTER 9

1 Danilo Türk is Professor of International Law, Faculty of Law, University in Ljubljana. He is currently Ambassador, Permanent Representative of Slovenia, to the UN. The views expressed are those of the author. This text is based on the oral presentation entitled 'The Right of Self-Determination' in the debate at the University of Warwick, Coventry, on 14 March, 1996.

2 Alain Pellet, *La Charte des Nations Unies* (Paris: Economica, 1991).
3 *Uti possidetis* is the principle according to which the administrative boundaries set by colonial powers are treated as the national boundaries of newly emergent nation-states and are held to be immutable.
4 Frederic Kirgis, 'The degrees of self-determination in the United Nations era', Editorial comment, *American Journal of International Law*, vol. 88, no. 2, April 1994, pp 304–11.

10

BETWEEN UNION AND SEPARATION: THE PATH OF CONCILIATION

Gidon Gottlieb[1]

In 1648, the Treaty of Westphalia consecrated in Europe a system of states which has been emulated throughout the planet. The Westphalian order was first and foremost territorial in nature; it reflected a system in which rulers were in full control of a defined territory and possessed absolute authority over its population. In our own times, the Westphalian order shows signs of strain: the weakening of the authority of the territorial state is especially noted. Yet the erosion of the power of the territorial state has not in political theory given rise to the elaboration of a post-Westphalian vision whose contours may already be perceived in the fog of contemporary events. A revision of the system of states has become necessary: the time may have come to make room for a system of nations and peoples side-by-side with the established system of territorial states, and in addition to it; the principle of territorial authority may have to be qualified; national and ethnic minorities do require arrangements verging on political independence that can be reconciled with conventional ideas on the sovereignty of the territorial states in which they dwell; the international status and privileges of these minorities must allow for a differentiated standing in international organisations.

The problem of minorities is an old one. In the first half of the twentieth century, it led the states of Europe to develop elaborate juridical arrangements for restive populations, and to do so without disrupting territorial integrity. The European juridical approach, enshrined in numerous treaties and declarations for 'the protection of minorities', involved a grant to individual persons who were members of minorities an array of rights that were supposed to safeguard their cultural and religious interests. By and large, these treaties were a dismal failure. In recent years, efforts to extend treaty rights to national or ethnic communities as such, and not merely to individuals, were defeated or side-tracked. In the 1990s, a modest initiative by Prince Hans Adam of Lichtenstein in the General Assembly of the United Nations led nowhere. In early 1999, the Rambouillet Conference failed to devise an agreed solution to the problem of ethnic Albanians, or to reconcile their claims with those of the former Republic of Yugoslavia. Yugoslavia remains the recognised sovereign in the province.

The repeated failure of treaties for the protection of minorities has swelled demands for self-determination, full independence and separation. The tide of separatist sentiment is felt in most multinational states – from Canada to Spain, Russia, China, India and the United Kingdom. In all these countries, subject national communities have become restive as past humiliations and injuries, real and imagined, sustain a torrent of resentment. The end of the Cold War has been accompanied by a resurgence of nationalisms of all kinds in the the quest for national identity and dignity.

Almost everywhere, the rise of the market and the decline of ideologies of the right and left have signalled a loss of faith in the capacity of the state to remedy social and personal ills. In Europe, the authority of nation-states has been buffeted both by the rise of the European Union and by the assertiveness of local and regional governments. Yet, paradoxically, the core demand of separatists is precisely the establishment of yet more national states, even as the institution of statehood is being emptied of much of what used to give it significance.

National identity has arisen to challenge the identity that state citizenship could once alone confer. Historic states can no longer ignore the determination of minorities to live free from what they regard as alien rule, but neither can they satisfy claims founded on national rights of all sorts: rights to a cultural heritage, rights to a historical homeland, and rights to its natural resources. Separation, an independent state, is the ultimate prize of nationalists, their banner is self-determination, and their demands are territorial. They regard devolution and autonomy as mere stepping stones to separation.

Dominant political theories present a stark set of choices for nationalists: either the achievement of some form of self-rule within the state from which they wish to part, or the establishment of a separate state. There is no third way, no generally accepted mode of political organisation to make room for the cultural and historical particularities of ethnic minorities. Nationalists know of no half-way-houses between subordination and equality, self-rule and independence.

The modern concept of the state is characterised by a striving for generality, by an aspiration to a uniform system of laws applicable to all persons and communities. Political theory in our time features general and uniform regimes for populations and territories irrespective of the wealth of particularities within them. Modern constitutional arrangements are notable for their uniformity across nations and cultures: in setting powers of the different branches of government, systems of election and appointments to posts, they display uniformity. There are few constitutional systems that abandon the ideal of uniformity and outline instead a patchwork of special regimes and particular forms of status responsive to the contours of local circumstances and historical accident. Where they do exist, such regimes are often regarded as anomalous relics of an earlier age, rather than as the wise accommodation of rival claims. For example, the complex maze of rights and privileges of the fractious Christian denominations in the Church of the Holy Sepulchre in Jerusalem, which developed across centuries of rivalry and strife, could hardly have emanated from the hands of a law-giver. The accommodations most likely to endure are those that grew custom-like, subject to constant revision and evolution. In political theory, however, the competing claims of custom and legislation were in the Western world largely resolved in favour of legislation, and of the uniformities that it implies. But legislated arrangements for subject peoples are not likely to last once coercive powers are eroded. A constitution or legislation that is not derived from respect for historic rights and claims will set the stage for future conflict and ultimate separation.

The very idea of the ethnic nation carries with it the seed of traumatic events: population transfers, territorial partition and ethnic cleansing. In the former USSR, as well as in Eastern and Balkan Europe, ethnic nationalism is feeding new demons that threaten the gains made for civilised values after the collapse of the Communist empire. The problem is the design of some intermediate status between politically subordinate autonomy on the one hand and fully sovereign statehood on the other: between the unity of territories and the rights of peoples. The gruesome bestiality of ethnic wars in Iraq, the former Yugoslavia, the former

Soviet Union and in a vast swath of other lands, has led to a reappraisal of the doctrine of self-determination. Distinguished thinkers now often regard self-determination as an 'evil'. After the Versailles Peace Conference, Robert Lansing, Woodrow Wilson's Secretary of State, lamented 'the danger of putting such an idea into the minds of certain races. It is bound to be the basis of impossible demands. The phrase is loaded with dynamite. What a calamity that the phrase was ever uttered.' Versailles probably did spawn – as we were warned – a real Frankenstein monster.

Close to 200 states, 3000 linguistic groups and 5000 national minorities form an awesome pattern of diversity and separateness, a planetary tower of Babel. Two hundred and thirty-three often restive peoples and national communities are said now to be advancing claims for self-determination. In the words of the former UN Secretary General, Boutros Ghali, 'if every ethnic, religious or linguistic group claimed statehood, there would be no limit to fragmentation, and peace, security and economic well-being for all, would become even more difficult to achieve'.

In Europe, fragmentation could undermine the peace of the continent. Scottish and Welsh separatism may ultimately lead to the break-up of the United Kingdom. This could threaten the stability of Europe. On the Continent, German influence would become preponderant, for until now the weight of a united Germany and of German-speaking peoples was balanced by the states on its periphery. The not inconceivable fragmentation of the United Kingdom would increase the relative weight of the new Germany. Other European nations like France and Russia might then try to redress the situation with consequences that no-one can foresee.

Great Britain has, again and again, displayed a genius for flexible constitutional design; it may yet find the way to retain Scotland within the realm while granting it a status that goes beyond self-rule. The rapid evolution of the European Union could facilitate the task. The Scots benefit from a triad of identities. They are citizens of the United Kingdom, bearers of passports of the European Union and members of the Scottish nation. Scottish identity may, however, require clearer expression. It involves not only the rights of individuals but also the collective status of the Scottish nation itself, both within the United Kingdom and within the European Union. A national regime for Scotland could, in addition to devolution and self-rule, also be based on special charters for cities and regions which recognise the particularities of each and place them for most local purposes beyond the reach of the parliament in Westminster. The laws of United Kingdom already provide for different kinds of British citizenship. British law could give more generous recognition to a Scottish nationality without prejudice to the legislation on United Kingdom citizenship. Moreover, in addition to self-rule, Scotland could be allowed a measure of international status in the European Union, the Commonwealth and other regional arenas. It will be recalled that the Ukraine and Byelorussia were once formally members of the United Nations alongside the Soviet Union, of which they were a constituent part. The hard issues involving the wealth of the North Sea could be addressed in some hybrid regime or ad hoc authority constituted of public and private interests.

An approach of this kind could have relevance for the future of Quebec, and of other countries troubled by the spectre of separatism. Symbolically potent solutions, conciliating union and independence, could offer a way out for nations that press for separation but do not want to break all links. Such nations should be given a chance to find their own good without causing the fragmentation or the break-up of the states they inhabit.

There is an evident danger in such arrangements. First, devolution and an international status of sorts can, when pushed to extremes, lead to the creation of a 'state within a state', with the potential discord and weakness that it implies. The responsibility for defence may have to remain the exclusive prerogative of the central government. The problem is compounded in small island states and mini-states that are becoming the more or less willing targets of money flows tied to the drug trade, to the Russian and other mafias, and to criminal activities of other kinds. The governments of even large states are known to have been tarnished by the drug trade. The control of deadly threats – such as the illicit trade in nuclear materials, terrorism and the spread of epidemics – would be greatly complicated in a world of many more small independent states. However, where small nations and communities are denied their culture and the exercise of their rights, the problem has a different hue. Separation and full independence may then be the only way out. The 'negative consensus' against fragmentation and Balkanisation cannot be allowed to block, in every case, the aspirations of nations desperate to free themselves from genocidal or tyrannical masters.

Contemporary practice points to a clear erosion of the notion of absolute sovereignty. The complex norms governing the European Union, the diverse layers of territorial arrangements contemplated in the two Oslo agreements between Israel and the Palestinians, the 'set of ideas' suggested for a settlement of the conflict in Cyprus, the 'declarations' governing efforts to settle the conflict in Northern Ireland all share the characteristic of blurring or qualifying principles of absolute territorial sovereignty which dominate public and specialist opinion. It is a paradox of our time that even as federations fare poorly and claims for separation become more intense, elaborate, highly complex collaborative solutions are advanced for intractable conflicts in the Balkans, in the former Soviet Union and in the Middle East. The Dayton Accords on the future of Bosnia illustrate how far states are willing to go in the realm of juridical fiction. The retention of the 'unity' of Bosnia as a single state can hardly mask its effective break-up into two countries and the legitimisation of Serb military gains. The skimpy powers granted to the future government of a 'united' Bosnia and the two hostile armies that will continue to face each other speak for themselves. The Dayton Accords cannot, in the long run, prevent the creation of close links between Serbia and Bosnian Serbs or between Croatia and the Croats in Bosnia. A distinction must be drawn between the constitutional accommodation of separatist claims designed to avert fragmentation, and diplomatic compromises of the kind reached in Dayton which merely paper over the reality of separation.

Conventional thinking about the nature of states continues to exercise its grip: state sovereignty means full control over both territory and people; sovereignty must be absolute, and all persons must be subject to the authority of the state. This doctrine informs political attitudes in many lands. It undermines efforts to shape a new order in which the state shares the political stage with other instrumentalities, whether supra-national, infra-national or non-territorial in character. The legitimacy and stability of opaque diplomatic arrangements for the disposition of separatist claims, and for the taming of ethnic conflicts, is sapped by the dominant brands of political thought. Intricate juridical regimes remain vulnerable for lack of public support, especially when the press, politicians and commentators hark back to the simple and definitive clarity of an era when authority over territories and peoples could be defined with precision and without ambiguity.

The time has come for an update, an *aggiornamento*, of the centuries-old doctrines about the nature of the state and the international society of states. The concept of sovereignty is in urgent need of deconstruction. It originated in an era in which the state was all-powerful and in which neither democratic principles nor human rights inhibited its ability to confront restive peoples. The need is apparent for new constitutional and doctrinal frameworks that conciliate between the notions of absolute sovereignty and state unity – between the integrity of states and claims for separation.

The agenda for such an *aggiornamento* is plain to see. The contemporary world order is based on sovereign states. The adjustment of this order, to make room for a society of nations alongside the system of states is a manageable task. A revision of the concept of sovereignty would permit different kinds of international status for territorial and non-territorial communities alike. It would lead to fresh thinking about functional territorial arrangements in disputed lands, as well as to new sets of concepts in regard to borders, national homes, citizenship, nationality and forms of association. It would, moreover, ease the path to new kinds of union among states and peoples.

Concepts, doctrines and frameworks are powerless by themselves to move nations and governments to real peace. The decisive weight of military force will unavoidably be reflected, as in Dayton, in the settlements reached, and the political will to resolve separatist and ethnic claims remains a precondition for their peaceful resolution. The cultivation of this political will requires the wise application of political, economic and even military leverage. But it also requires a vision of a future in which nations are not required to disown aspirations on whose altar blood has been shed and martyrs created. The stability of agreements ultimately depends on the conviction that they were not merely necessary, but that they were also just.

NOTE ON CHAPTER 10

1 Gidon Gottlieb holds the Leo Spitz Chair of International Law and Diplomacy in the University of Chicago. He is the author of *Nation against State: A New Approach to Ethnic Conflicts and the Decline of Sovereignty* (New York: Council on Foreign Relations, 1993). This paper is based on a lecture given at Warwick University on 22 November 1995.

11

DOES A NATION NEED A STATE? REFLECTIONS ON LIBERAL NATIONALISM

Neil MacCormick[1]

ON NATIONALISMS

What is it that makes a 'nation' or a 'country', in the sense of a place to which a person might belong, and not just a territory arbitrarily marked on a map? Two ways of thinking about this have gained prominence in contemporary discussions. One way stresses civic institutions, public offices, public agencies and officials, churches in their secular activities, and common and authoritative rules with a territorial scope. These define a country and the nation that inhabits it. The other way stresses common ethnicity and culture, a shared language perhaps, a shared history and common ancestral struggles. The nation is the community of fate, the community of ethnic bonds.

The models need not be interpreted as exclusive. Civic institutions can generate and become a focus of common culture; cultural identity can lead to a demand for common civic institutions, or the adaptation of non-civic institutions to civic purposes (consider the Catholic Church in Polish history). Real countries and nations may fall nearer one pole or the other.

In parallel, political thinkers propose two ideal types of nationalism. Civic nationalism seeks to constitute under a sense of common belonging those who share civic institutions, linking them together under a common appeal to what Jürgen Habermas has called 'constitutional patriotism', and to treat the nation as open to all who come under and accept the jurisdiction of the civic institutions.[2] Ethnic nationalism focuses on the self-determination of the historically given – perhaps even genetically given – community of culture and of ancestral belonging.

Again, it would be wrong, though it is not uncommon, to treat these ideal types as mutually exclusive. Clearly, a sense of loyalty to historically continuous institutions gives a sense of belonging to the historically extended community which has shared the institutions, and the cultural, ethnic and linguistic traditions that have flourished in the historically extended community. Likewise, where an ethnically conscious group has developed its own institutions, it can extend an opportunity of belonging, by adoption as it were, to newcomers who accept them.

A much-argued issue is whether either version of nationalism can in any form be shaped into an acceptable political principle, and whether either can be accepted within a broadly liberal framework. The argument I shall put is in favour of acknowledging and supporting a certain approach to nationalism under the name 'liberal nationalism'. I do so from the standpoint of a long-term activist in the Scottish National Party. Let me start simply with the thought that a predominantly civic conception of nationalism might be applied to defending the survival and distinctiveness of a country's civic institutions and the cultural values and practices that surround them. This would require some political recognition of the nation in question, ideally including self-governing political institutions.

NATIONS AS STATES?

The key question is whether the self-governing political institutions that a self-respecting nation ought to have must necessarily be the institutions of a fully sovereign state. 'Must all nations be or become state-nations?' we have to ask; and conversely, 'Must all states be or become nation-states? Does a multinational state like the United Kingdom have to become a one-nation state or forfeit its authenticity as a state?'

The context of the debate is set by Gidon Gottlieb in his *Nation against State*.[3] He argues that the world we confront inevitably contains more nations than states. The human beings who identify themselves as belonging to nations (whether toward the civic or the ethnic pole of identity), and the nations that emerge from these processes of identification, occupy states that do not match the nations in their totality. Moreover, it would be quite impossible to bring about any easy matching of states and nations. For, on any reasonable definition of what counts as a nation, there are simply too many nations too dispersed, and they are too oddly distributed geographically for the international order of states to accommodate them comfortably. Too many boundaries would require too drastic revision, too many minorities would persist in too many settings even after revision, for there to be the remotest possibility of peacefully resolving the states-and-nations question in such a way as to match up a single territorial state to each nation. There would have to be many boundary-shifts and ethnic cleansings before any one-to-one pattern could be settled.

Yet nationalism, as Gottlieb says, is one of the stubbornest facts of contemporary political life. The collapse of communism and the end of the adversarial geopolitics of the Cold War have revealed a world in which national and nationalistic aspirations have grown in intensity, not withered away. To achieve a peaceful world order, the statespersons of the world must address themselves to this problem.

One possibility is that of opposition: discount national aspirations as atavistic and tribalistic, and encourage everyone to take her or his place in the states that there happen to be. So long, however, as the states that exist advertise themselves as, and legitimate themselves through, the rhetoric of the 'nation-state', this is a disingenuous response. For 'nation-states' are all too often states in the image of one particular dominant nation or nationality within the state, and minorities in them are put on the cleft stick of denying their own identity for the sake of full citizenship or asserting their identity at the price of non-recognition or non-participation as full citizens.

Another possibility is simple denial, simple aversion of the gaze; this is the posture traditionally, if erroneously, ascribed to the ostrich. Ostriches in our context refuse to acknowledge that there are any real problems properly describable as problems of nationality; the real underlying problems are different and should be handled without regard to tiresome claims about nation and nationality, except insofar as the 'nation' is taken to be a synonym of some recognised state. The ostrich's trouble, in this as in other cases, is that the phenomenon from which one averts one's gaze does not go away. Indeed it may become the more threatening and virulent for being ignored.

The third possibility is to seek a radical solution, acknowledging the legitimacy of national complaints and national aspirations, especially those of the excluded nationalities. But the solution favoured cannot be what is often the preferred option for the unrepresented or unrecognised nationalities, namely that each should have a sovereign state of its own. By the initial hypothesis announced above, this is simply impossible. This, of course, is Gottlieb's line. He wants to de-couple nation from state and give nations proper recognition – passports, national homelands, cultural representation – apart from states. The boundaries of states should stay more-or-less as given, and states should remain the basic guarantors of civil peace and economic organisation, nowadays in a framework of international law that guarantees human rights and that facilitates free trade and commerce. Within and across these boundaries, nations must be given their due recognition, albeit at the cost of some pretensions historically asserted by 'nation-states'.

This is in many respects a generous vision, and one with which I find myself quite largely in agreement. As expressed in some recent papers, my own inclination has been to start from a European (though I think not an unduly Euro-centric) perspective, and to reflect on the way in which the development hitherto of European communities and European union has led to a transcendence of the traditional conception of state sovereignty. This development sets not-fully-sovereign member states within the framework of a legal and political community, now union, which itself lacks the attributes of a sovereign federal union and seems unlikely to acquire them in the foreseeable future. The still-embryonic doctrine of subsidiarity, as a doctrine of the European constitutional order, seems to promise a way forward in which different layers of communality can flourish politically and be accorded the legal authority to conduct at a local level that range of decision-making that is best exercised at the local level, informed by local knowledge and understanding.

If it is true that Europe is now blazing a trail 'beyond the sovereign state', then we are perhaps establishing the kind of framework that would be essential for moving forward seriously with a project such as Gottlieb's. Those who invented and exported to the rest of the world the idea of the independent political society as a sovereign state are now building in a somewhat intuitive way a successor model for political and economic co-operation which keeps the state – now as a member-state rather than sovereign nation-state – but locates it in a legal order of co-operative rather than fully independent decision-making. Especially when this is coupled with the obligations towards human rights that are policed through the European Convention and the Commission and Court of Human Rights, the stage seems well set for a reasonably full-blooded acknowledgement of the rights and aspirations of nations contained within, or crossing the borders of, member-states. There have been substantial moves in this direction, for example in the autonomous regions of Spain, among the several self-governing communities of Belgium, in the relationship of Corsica to France, and also in the case of some regions and islands in Italy.

One can cite the European Community Treaty as giving a pointer in the relevant direction. In Article 128.1, it provides:

> The Community shall contribute to the flowering of the cultures of the Member States, while respecting their national and regional diversity and at the same time bringing the common cultural heritage to the fore.

This points to the possibility of a common European patriotism which focuses both on the historic riches of a European culture that is also regional in character, and on a constitutional framework that encourages self-government and civic patriotism at and below the level of member states – all in accordance with the principle of subsidiarity now written into the Union Treaty.

NATIONALISM AFTER SOVEREIGNTY

These developments point to the growth of a political context highly favourable to the general thesis propounded by Gottlieb. In the Europe of the European Union we confront a politics 'beyond the sovereign state'. Old conceptions of state-sovereignty and of the absolutism of the nation-state are obsolete. This does not abolish either states or nations as politico-cultural communities. Nor, therefore, does it necessarily abolish nationalism. Opposition to the new order can arise from certain forms of nationalism that are wedded to two particular ideas: that every nation must be a sovereign state, and that every sovereign state should inculcate actively in its citizens a one-nation civic nationalism. This view, which I reject, I shall here name 'sovereign-state nationalism', associating it with Conservative Euro-scepticism in the United Kingdom and elsewhere.

The issue is whether there is any more acceptable nationalism to set against sovereign-state nationalism. I think there is. What I propose goes by the name of 'liberal nationalism'. It is to the new politics after sovereignty that we owe the scope for this new nationalism, an acceptable and even perhaps mandatory nationalism intrinsically liberal in character. I am not alone in arguing for this; indeed I do so in the shadow of, and with deep indebtedness to, Yael Tamir, who argues for it in her book *Liberal Nationalism*.[4] The argument acknowledges that nationalisms of various kinds, set in various political contexts, are a prominent feature of the contemporary world, and it also acknowledges the problematic character of nationalism from the standpoint of liberal values. For liberalism requires (at least) a universalistic view of the rights to be enjoyed by human beings, while any nationalism involves an engagement with some form of particularism, reserving particular rights, eg of residence in a territory or political participation in a government or perhaps many other still more advantageous rights, to members of the nation in question, and reserving different treatment for outsiders.

This contradiction is, however, more apparent than real, since one can universally prescribe that everyone is entitled to particularistic rights, like the right to participate in the life of their own family, or the right to participate in a self-determining national community. Much more problematic would be to prescribe such particularistic rights as an absolute and peremptory entitlement, given the world as it is. The price of universalisation is acceptance of each universal norm as a principle to be weighed along with others, not as a moral or political absolute. The challenge, from a nationalist point of view, is also a putatively liberal one: it is to define the content of a nationalist principle or principles in a satisfactorily universalistic way, and to assign some less than absolute weight to the principles so enunciated, but to do so in such a way as not to trivialise the principles asserted.

As a working idea in the rest of this paper, I shall work towards the following as my version of the liberal nationalist principle:

> the members of a nation are as such and in principle entitled to effective organs of political self-government within the world order of sovereign or post-sovereign states; but these need not provide for self-government in the form of a sovereign state.[5]

The identity of the nation is conceived primarily in civic terms, though it is to be acknowledged that this will also draw in elements of the cultural and the ethnic; these latter are accepted only to the extent that they are compatible with the other constraints for which I argue.

Needless to say, liberalism is a much-contested concept or family of political ideas and programmes. But two principles or attitudes should be seen as fundamental for anything credibly recognisable as belonging to the family of liberal thought. These are universalism and individualism. Let me take for granted universalism, as a formal principle of the kind hinted at above, and add to it a corollary of a kind that frees it of its purely formal character, namely that in framing the categories that we treat as universalisable, there always ought to be a presumption in favour of more inclusive over less inclusive categories. The burden of argumentation rests always on those who assert narrower categories and can be satisfied only by adducing genuine functional appropriateness. Thus 'all qualified drivers may use motor vehicles on public roads' is a narrower principle than 'all human beings may use motor vehicles on public roads'; but given further assumptions about the value of safety and the relevance of driving tests to safe driving, the less inclusive category is here justified.

The individualistic element in the proposed version of liberalism has two internal principles: the first makes an assumption about value, namely that nothing can be deemed a fundamental human good unless it is capable of being enjoyed as an enhancement of life by a human being as a distinct individual; the second makes an assumption of value, namely that a social situation in which human individuals have scope for self-development and self-realisation through autonomous decisions and choices, taken either individually or in free collaboration with others, is of value both to the self-realising individuals and to others. Of these principles, the former rejects the claims on behalf of superhuman or collectively-human entities to be repositories of ultimate human values – there cannot, for example, be 'national values' enjoyed by nations as such but incapable of being enjoyed or experienced as values by human individuals as individuals. The latter asserts a particular claim on behalf of individuals: there is special political value in securing a social situation where self-aware individuality and self-fulfilment are possible for individuals.

Individualism so characterised ought to be dubbed 'value-individualism', and to be distinguished from what is sometimes called 'methodological individualism'. This latter, I understand, postulates that there are individual human beings whose character as such is independent of any social location or setting and that anything which can be predicated about society or community or human beings collectively is reducible either to predicates about individuals severally or to some averaging statement about individuals in the aggregate. This is a quite untenable belief. For we are all, as Yael Tamir puts it, 'contextual individuals', and the context is that of some cultural grouping, some social location. The individual is no more intelligible apart from society than society is intelligible save by reference to interacting individuals.

Despite appearances, the idea that humans are contextual individuals is not hostile to the idea that they can be autonomous moral agents. On the contrary, they can be autonomous moral agents, but to become this requires the support of appropriate social conditions. This is a thesis that connects us back to 'value-individualism': the thesis that there is special, indeed unique, value in human individuality and a special value of those forms of human social organisation that foster individuality and autonomy. It is the opposite of the thesis that individuality is just ontologically given.

In liberalism as here understood, the most credible candidate for being a fundamental principle of substantive morality, and thus also of politics, is that of respect for persons. We are to respect each human being as a distinct individual, with all that goes into his or her constitution as such. But if that is so, it behoves us also to recognise that, as was just argued, all individuals are necessarily contextual; hence in respecting individuals, we are committed to respecting what enables persons to have self-understanding and self-respect as individuals, though always under the qualification that no particular individual can be entitled to conditions of self-respect that are incompatible with the self-respect of others. This shows what is so fundamentally unacceptable about disparagement of individuals on such grounds as nationality, ethnicity or gender.

Let us now suppose, as seems to be true, that a sense of national identity and belonging does for a very large part of the present population of the world play an important part in individuals' self-understanding. Contextual individuals may have as one among their most significant contexts some national identity. To that extent, respect for national identities, and commitment in principle to the nationalist principle stated above, are not merely not incompatible with liberalism, but are actually required by it.

The liberal nationalist principle as stated above has as its first limb the following:

> the members of a nation are as such and in principle entitled to effective organs of political self-government within the world order of sovereign or post-sovereign states.

Given the primacy ascribed to the civic conception of membership of a nation, this seems to me to be a wholly acceptable principle from a liberal point of view. It is of course important to remember that it is a principle, not an absolute rule. This means that in any real-life situation there may be competing principles, such that it is a question of weighing and balancing how far and in what ways our principle is susceptible of implementation without injury to equally important, or more important, values and principles. It is also subject to constraints of time, place and circumstance. Therefore it is correct to add the second limb and state the principle in full as:

> the members of a nation are as such in principle entitled to effective organs of political self-government within the world order of sovereign or post-sovereign states; but these need not provide for self-government in the form of a sovereign state.[6]

CODA: SCOTLAND AND NATIONALISM

I ought to append at least some summary observations on the position I take as a member of the Scottish National Party, indeed as a recidivist parliamentary candidate under its colours, which I have carried in the elections of 1979, 1983, 1987, 1992 and 1997. How do I see that the principles I have stated apply to Scotland in relation to the United Kingdom?

There are several ways of perceiving the United Kingdom. One, much in use, is to see it as a classical 'nation-state', in which it makes perfect sense to advocate 'one nation' policies, as do some Conservatives. This draws on the long history of a common British monarchy, the sovereignty of a unitary crown in a unitary parliament that is custodian of an unwritten constitution rooted in convention, custom and common law. The divisions that have mattered have been divisions of class and the effort has been to transcend such divisions in order to reconstitute, or constitute, a single nation of shared interest and sympathy beyond differences of social class and economic prosperity.

The trouble is that this vision is by no means uncontested. There is a different perception available of the constitution, which points out that first Great Britain, and then the United Kingdom of Great Britain and Ireland, and since 1922 the United Kingdom of Great Britain and Northern Ireland, were constituted by agreed Articles of Union bringing together pre-existing legal and political entities into a new union, but deliberately not homogenising the parts. Although a unitary crown and parliament were set up, other important organs of state were quite deliberately kept distinct: there remained different established churches, different systems of law and of the administration of justice, different forms of local government and different educational systems. Moreover, in the union between Scotland and England, provision was made to secure the continuing distinctiveness of these Scottish institutions, and that provision was expressed as fundamental and essential to the continuing legitimacy of union. So our constitution, though incorporating much from English common law and constitutional custom, is nevertheless not aboriginal and unwritten, but the result of solemn agreements made in 1707 and 1801, subsequently amended to accommodate the secession of the larger part of Ireland, and certain other matters.[7]

The one-nation thesis is in effect predicated on a picture of the United Kingdom as England writ large. Both inside and outside the United Kingdom it has been argued, or more often just assumed, that Scotland, and for a while Ireland, were added or annexed to England, albeit by treaty rather than by conquest in the Scottish case, and that while local or 'regional' distinctiveness survives to a greater or lesser extent, these are historical survivals, or sops to local sentiment allowed by the tolerance of the sovereign parliament. There is one nation, essentially England, with fringe additions.

An opposed view reads the historical and constitutional record as the constituting of a multinational state, originating in a dynastic union of a kind quite familiar in Europe. Within the unitary state, different national traditions and institutions survive, although of course the metropolitan tradition is that of the larger and more prosperous party. From this point of view, the one-nation thesis, although generous and inclusivist in its ambition, is effectively also imperialistic in the assimilation of the lesser nationalities into the greater.

In general, the multinational perception of Britain seems to prevail in Scotland, where people by a considerable majority, regardless of party affiliation, characterise themselves as Scottish as their primary identification, and British only in a secondary way. Even those most attached to the present Union, when articulating the case for it, present the special virtue of the union as being that it gives full scope to the preservation, strength and development of Scottish civic institutions and cultural inheritances, while preserving opportunities for co-operation and participation in a powerful unitary state whose strength consists in its hospitality to several national traditions. Scots law is not under threat, nor the Scottish educational system, nor distinctive institutions of local government, nor the Church of Scotland, but these civic institutions belong to people whose prosperity and opportunity for influence in the world are enhanced, not weakened, by full membership in a United Kingdom.

This view is not universally accepted, of course. It fails to acknowledge the need for an effective internal democracy, say critics. Scottish representation in the union is in effect at the pleasure of the executive branch of government, through a Secretary of State for Scotland who is necessarily the appointee of the British Prime Minister and representative of the UK majority party in the UK parliament, and not the leader of a Scottish majority which may differ – and indeed often does differ – from the UK majority.

This critique leads to the contemporary demand for a substantial degree of legislative and parliamentary devolution to Scotland, albeit still within a United Kingdom whose unitary parliament remains the ultimate authority on all matters of irreducibly common interest to the whole UK. Keep defence, foreign affairs, representation in Europe, macroeconomic policy and most aspects of taxation as all-UK responsibilities, but establish in Scotland a local parliament, with an executive answerable to it, to handle all other matters concerning peace, order and good government. Let this parliament have minor taxation powers to secure funding for local initiatives, but finance it mainly with block grants from the UK treasury. This is the solution now embodied in the Scotland Act 1998 in operation since early summer 1999, with the election of the first Scottish parliament since 1707.

There are serious difficulties with this solution. Unless there is to be parallel devolution to other constituent countries, England as well as Wales and Northern Ireland, there will be an obvious imbalance of representation in the UK parliament, where Scottish MPs can vote in relation to England on issues like education, water supply arrangements. transport and the like, while on those issues in Scotland, neither English MPs nor indeed Scottish members of the UK parliament will retain legislative competence in the ordinary way. Equally, a limited power of taxation in supplementation of a block grant will invite all sorts of potential conflict and manipulation of the block grant so as to cancel budgetary independence. To resolve these difficulties, it might be necessary to call for the establishment either of an all-England parliament or of English regional parliaments, neither of which seems likely to occur or to be workable in the face of massive absence of demand for such developments from the people of England. It remains to be seen whether the British genius for compromise will make work in practice a scheme which in theory seems fraught with difficulty.

The remaining possibility is to look for continuing union among the parts of the British Isles primarily via the European Union and Community rather than by internal federation or quasi-federation. This is the project of 'independence in Europe' advocated by the Scottish National Party, and enjoying very considerable support, though (as of June 1999) still some distance short of an overall majority, in Scotland. The status of independent member states within the confederal union that is evolving in Western Europe and steadily extending its bounds, resolves the democratic deficit of incorporating union without incurring the difficulties specific to devolution. It might well be supplemented by the Council of the Isles set up following the Good Friday Agreement of 1998. It, therefore, appears the most eligible of the options compatible with liberal nationalism. But this is a question of judgement on the balance of advantage overall. Each of the options is indeed compatible with the principle of liberal nationalism – and thus also with the spirit of Gottliebís approach.

NOTES ON CHAPTER 11

1 Neil MacCormick is Regius Professor of Law at the University of Edinburgh. He is author of many scholarly books and articles, including *The Scottish Debate: Essays on Scottish Nationalism* (London: OUP, 1970); *Legal Right and Social Democracy* (Oxford: Clarendon Press, 1982); *An Institutional Theory of Law* (with O. Weinberger) (Dordrecht: D. Reidel, 1986).

2 See Jürgen Habermas, *Between Facts and Norms*, (Cambridge: Polity, 1997), appendix 11, 'Citizenship and National Identity' (first published in 1991).

3 Gidon Gottlieb, *Nation against State* (New York: Council on Foreign Relations Press, 1993).

4 Yael Tamir, *Liberal Nationalism*, (Princeton: Princeton University Press, 1993). My argument is further developed in my *Legal Right and Social Democracy* (Oxford: Clarendon Press, 1982), ch. 13 'Nation and Nationalism'; N. MacCormick and O. Weinberger, *An Institutional Theory of Law* (Dordrecht: D. Reidel, 1986), ch. 8, ' Institutional Morality and the Constitution'; W. Twining (ed.), *Issues of Self-Determination* (Aberdeen: Aberdeen University Press, 1991), ch. 2, 'Is Nationalism Philosophically Credible?'; 'Beyond the Sovereign State', *Modern Law Review* 56, 1993, pp 1–23; 'What Place for Nationalism in the Modern World' in Hume Papers on Public Policy, 2, 1994, pp 79–95; 'The Maastricht-Urteil: Sovereignty Now', *European Law Journal* 1, 1995, pp 259–66; 'Sovereignty: Myth and Reality' in *Towards Universal Law* (Uppsala: Iustus Vörlag, 1995) (*De Lege*, Juridiska Fakulteten I Uppsala, Yearbook, 5th year 1995); 'Liberalism, Nationalism, and the Post-Sovereign State', *Political Studies*, special issue, 1996 (ed. R. Bellamy and D. Castiglione).

5 My argument is further developed in N. MacCormick, *Legal Right and Social Democracy* (Oxford: Clarendon Press, 1982), ch. 13, 'Nation and Nationalism'; N. MacCormick and O. Weinberger, *An Institutional Theory of Law* (Dordrecht: D. Reidel, 1986), ch. 8, 'Institutional Morality and the Constitution'; W. Twining (ed.), *Issues of Self-Determination* (Aberdeen: Aberdeen University Press, 1991), ch. 2, 'Is Nationalism Philosophically Credible?'; 'Beyond the Sovereign State', *Modern Law Review* 56, 1993, pp 1–23; 'What Place for Nationalism in the Modern World' in *Hume Papers on Public Policy* 2, 1994, pp 79–95; 'The Maastricht-Urteil: Sovereignty Now' in *European Law Journal* 1, 1995, pp 259–66; 'Sovereignty: Myth and Reality' in *Towards Universal Law* (Uppsala: Iustus Vörlag, 1995) (De Lege, Juridiska Fakulteten I Uppsala, Yearbook, 5th year, 1995); 'Liberalism, Nationalism, and the Post-Sovereign State' in *Political Studies*, special issue, 1996 (ed. R. Bellamy and D. Castiglione).

6 The argument I am putting here is, by a different route, fully compatible with the theses propounded by Gidon Gottlieb in his *Nation against State*.

7 See McCormick, 'The English Constitution, the British State and the Scottish Anomaly' (1997 British Academy Lecture), *Scottish Affairs*, Special Issue, 'Understanding Constitutional Change', Edinburgh, 1998, pp 129–145.

PART V

CIVIC NATIONALISM

12

BENIGN NATIONALISM? THE POSSIBILITIES OF THE CIVIC IDEAL

Michael Ignatieff[1]

Some questions imply their own answer. 'Is there a benign nationalism?' implies that there isn't. At least it suggests that if nationalism does have benign aspects such as love of country, these cannot be separated from their malign results: violence, territorial conquest or chauvinism. So the question seems to come down to this: can you have the good consequences of nationalism – love of country, national solidarity, willingness to sacrifice yourself for one's nation – without the malign ones as well – intolerance, violence and conquest?

If we distinguish between patriotism and nationalism, our difficulties appear to be resolved. We could call patriotism the benign sort of nationalism and end the matter there, since most, though not all, people think that there are morally respectable forms of patriotism. Of course it remains the last refuge of a scoundrel, as Samuel Johnson said, but only when it is offered as an excuse for the behaviour of scoundrels.

But redefining terms is a linguistic subterfuge. For the question remains: can you have patriotism without nationalism? Can you have the good without the bad? And is the good so very good if it seems invariably to entail the bad?

We tend to use these words with narcissistic imprecision, reserving the word patriotism for our own pride in our country, while using nationalism to stigmatise the baleful chauvinism of others. Thus Americans, British and French people are patriotic; Serbs, Croats and Bosnians are nationalistic. Our emotions, because they are ours, must be benign; theirs, because they are theirs, must be malign.

A less self-regarding way to sharpen up the distinction between patriotism and nationalism is to observe that a patriot invariably loves a country which already exists, whereas a nationalist often loves a country which does not. Patriotism is the privilege of those with states; it is benign simply because it is privileged. Nationalism is the language of the stateless, the unwilling imperial subject, the subjugated minority. Nationalism is the claim that such people, by virtue of their language, tradition, ethnicity, race or religion deserve to be called a nation; and because they deserve to be called a nation, they deserve a state of their own. They deserve a state, so the argument goes, either because they cannot be safe without one, or because, less precisely, they cannot flourish as a people without a state to call their own. Most claims to self-determination of this sort inherently entail conflict. Because nationalism is usually the claim of a nation to a state which it does not yet possess, it may be ethically defensible but it cannot, by definition, be benign. To achieve its aims it must, and usually does, fight.

Another way to deal with the problem of distinguishing between patriotism and nationalism is to pronounce oneself a cosmopolitan and declare the dispute irrelevant. A cosmopolitan looks with disdain on patriotism and nationalism alike; stands above the melee and defends universal values against national ones. There are at least three kinds of cosmopolitan. Marxist cosmopolitans stand for the brotherhood of working men or the brotherhood of oppressed colonial peoples against various forms of reactionary nationalism; gentlemanly cosmopolitans pronounce themselves at home in all civilised places and regard nationalism as a vulgar bourgeois prejudice; and liberal cosmopolitans proclaim their adherence to universal human standards rather than national cultural traditions. For all three types of cosmopolitan, a 'benign' nationalism is a contradiction in terms.

My difficulty with cosmopolitanism – aristocratic, Marxist and liberal – is that it is the privilege of those who can take their own membership in secure nation-states for granted. It is easy to disdain the vulgar, strident or chauvinist logic of nationalism if one already possesses the right to have a passport of one's own. What nationalists seem to understand more clearly than cosmopolitans is that the right to have any rights at all only inheres in those who have a state. This is not to deny that states commonly oppress their citizens or that there must be extra-national instruments, like the European Conventions and the Universal Declaration on Human Rights, to override national jurisdictions in certain instances, and thus to protect the rights human beings have as human beings. The fact remains that such protection as our human rights enjoy derive more from our citizenship in viable states than from our membership of a common species or from organisations like the United Nations. The modern state remains the instrument of first resort for the protection of peoples' right to security from foreign and domestic violence. Globalisation may reduce the economic sovereignty of nations; and international law may be chipping away at the inviolability of states – both of these are positive developments, in my view; but both globalisation and the internationalisation of human rights standards and protections redouble rather than reduce the need for legitimate nation-states capable of affording human beings the essential security they require in order to enjoy any stable human rights protection at all.

So the question is not, as cosmopolitans suppose, how to transcend nationalism. It is rather how are we to retain the good in nationalism: cohesive national communities and legitimate nation-states, without the bad – aggression, chauvinism and war?

In *Blood and Belonging*, I tried to move beyond a certain narcissism which contrasts 'our' patriotism and 'their' nationalism, especially in regard to ethnic war in Eastern Europe.[2] I tried instead to distinguish between civic and ethnic nationalism, between forms of nationalism which appeal to people on the basis of ethnicity, language, religion or race, and those forms which appeal to people on the basis of shared allegiance to certain constitutional principles.

Robert Fine has criticised me for implying that if nationalism is 'civic' it must be by definition benign. Calling both of these forms of allegiance 'nationalism' means – by implication – that neither are necessarily 'benign'.[3] America, Britain and France each qualify as examples of 'civic nationalist' societies, that is societies built on allegiance to constitutional or republican principles rather than common ethnicity. Each one has been remarkably malign, at various times, to minorities within its ranks and aggressive towards enemies beyond. The British nation-state was created in the bloody conquest of Ireland and the subjugation of Scotland. American civic nationalism was forged in the crucible of civil war. From the Palmer Raids of the 1920s to McCarthyism in the 1950s, American patriotism has been recurrently hijacked by paranoid demagogues and turned into a hectoring language of intimidation. The liberal voices which maintained that the

Jeffersonian terms of civic inclusion in American life did not need to be turned into a loyalty test were swept aside. Such episodes indicate that the civic identity of a nation is not 'above' politics or ideology. Its terms can be hijacked by faction, distorted by demagogues and banalised by sentimentality. 'Civic' language can be turned against dissidents and minorities just as 'ethnic' language can.

Likewise, French revolutionary nationalism may have been insistently 'civic' in its definition of national identity on the basis of Liberty, Equality and Fraternity, but these very civic values underwrote the messianic imperialism of Napoleon and the French revolutionary armies. As in the American case, there is no necessary relation between the 'civic' character of the national identity and peaceful behaviour towards foreign nations and neighbours. Indeed, nations like France and America which have believed, at least at certain times, that their particular brand of 'civic' contract deserved to be exported to the entire human race have proved to be a menace to international order.

'Civic' in other words doesn't necessarily mean 'benign', especially when the elites of the society in question are all taken from the same class or ethnic group. In societies where a majority ethnic group defines the content of national symbols and traditions to the exclusion of others, it is easy for 'civic' values to become an instrument of oppression. One feature of the national histories of France, America and Britain which we are just beginning to appreciate is the extent to which their 'civic constitutionalism' was forged within unchallenged and unquestioned assumptions about their social and cultural homogeneity. Liberty, Equality and Fraternity were intended for white, propertied French males; British parliamentary democracy likewise; and if the American franchise was, at its origins, drawn wider in Jacksonian America than in Victorian Britain, it still excluded blacks and women. In such societies, therefore, civic contractualism rested, in effect, on a social and cultural homogeneity enforced by civic exclusion.

From the 1870s onwards in all three societies these civic exclusions were successfully challenged: first all adult males, then women, then blacks and other visible minorities, then adolescents were formally granted the right to vote and hold office. We forget how recently this struggle for inclusion has been concluded. If we take the American Civil Rights Voting Act of 1965 as the conclusion of the formal struggle, we can see that it is only within our own lifetimes that the idea of civic contractualism for all has been achieved. In this sense, a fully civic nationalism has only become possible in these societies within our lifetimes.

Given the social, cultural, sexual, religious and ethnic heterogeneity of most modern societies, civic contractualism is the only possible basis for the national solidarity and social cohesion which we rightly praise as the positive side of nationalism. This is not to imply that new arrivals cannot identify with many of the traditional ethnically derived symbols of national pride. Indeed 'becoming more English than the English' is a frequent spiritual trajectory of many assimilating immigrants, at least in the past. Yet there are certain elements of the ethno-religious heritage of a country – an established church, or a parliament largely, if not exclusively, open to whites – which it is difficult, if not impossible, for a non-Christian or non-white migrant to identify with. These symbols need changing, or a society risks losing the active allegiance of a portion of its population. The alteration required is to ground the symbols in civic values with which all can easily identify. Of course, it is apparent that all 'civic' societies have betrayed their ideals. Nowhere does the practice of civic incorporation correspond to the ideal. But at least these societies possess ideals: in France, liberty, equality and fraternity; in America, equal protection before the law; in Britain, due process and legal fairness. In societies based on the principle of ethnic or religious majority rule, the rights of minorities are inherently less secure.

The difficulty with the distinction is that most 'civic' nationalist societies depend on certain 'ethnic' elements to sustain nationalist commitment; while most 'ethnic' societies ostensibly safeguard a host of 'civic' principles. In the case of Britain, for example, most British people might be surprised to think of themselves as a case of the 'civic nationalist' paradigm. Asked why they love their country, they would be more likely to respond with 'ethnic' than 'civic' answers, citing the 'English way of life', Shakespeare, the separate island destiny, the food and the weather, rather than parliamentary democracy, an independent judiciary and the rule of law. In an ethnic majority nation-state like Croatia, liberal-minded Croatians, when asked to say why they love their country would certainly cite the language, customs and religion of the Croatian people, but they would also stress Croatia's adherence to certain human rights norms and its democratic constitution. So the distinction between 'civic' and 'ethnic' is muddy. Most allegiance fuses the two. If so, the ideal of differentiating the 'civic' side of nationalism from the 'ethnic' might seem hopeless. Better to make peace with both strands in our allegiance: our devotion to certain principles, which are universals and our love of the particular. On such an account nationalism is always a mixture of the two: it is folly to disentangle them.

This might be true if civic nation-states happened to be mono-ethnic or mono-religious in their composition. Some are. Thanks to its efficient ethnic cleansing of its Serbian ethnic minority,

Croatia is now very nearly an ethnically homogenous nation-state. In these conditions, the ethnic is bound to dominate the civic in the components of national pride. Indeed, the removal of its ethnic minority may so weaken the civic components of Croatian identity that its democracy may be in danger. It is not accidental that a nation which engages in ethnic cleansing in order to make itself free ends up not as a true democracy but as a plebiscitary dictatorship.

It does not follow from the Croatian example that nations composed largely of a single ethnic group are necessarily less democratic because of it. The demography of modern Poland is the work of Nazi genocide and the Soviet-American allocation of borders after World War II. The demography of the modern Czech Republic is the result of the forced transfer of the Sudeten Germans together with the divorce with the Slovaks. Both nations are now ethnically homogenous, though for reasons which both Poles and Czechs have reason to lament. Neither are they less democratic for being composed of single ethnic groups. Indeed their particularly tragic heritage from World War II makes their leadership – especially Vaclav Havel – attentive to the necessity of keeping true to the civic heritage of democratic and republican values.

But mono-ethnic nation-states are now the exception rather than the rule. Most other Western European and North American democracies are composed of many different ethnic, religious, national or racial groups who do not, by definition, subscribe to exactly the same national mythologies or sources of pride. They do no eat the same food, practice the same way of life, read the same classics of national literature, or even share the same immemorial enemies. Common ethnicity no longer provides the glue which bonds the nation to the state and vice versa.

In such contexts the question of national cohesion arises. By cohesion, I mean the governability of these societies, the willingness of individuals and interest groups to compromise with each other, to abide by the rule of law, to participate actively in political and social life, and on occasion to respond to calls by the elite for restraint or sacrifice.

This is a deliberately 'thin' definition of national cohesion. There are 'thicker' ones on offer: the demand that ethnic groups assimilate into the culture of the majority; that they identify with a certain way of life, and that their values reflect those of the majority. Liberals – and I am one – defend 'thin' measures of national cohesion, believing that 'thicker' ones, largely defended by conservatives and sometimes by socialists, potentially compromise the civic contract of the host society itself, namely its commitment to allow individuals to shape their values and lives as they see fit, provided these choices do not significantly endanger the rights of others.

Arriving ethnic groups can establish themselves and live in peace in our societies without dislodging the dominant ethnic majority from its traditional role in defining national mythologies. Britain is a multicultural society whose ruling mythologies remain not merely white but English and whose nationalism, therefore, is imbued with a strong ethnic tinge. Despite the fact that the Union is now several centuries old, it is not in the self-understandings of many British people that they belong to a multinational state. Nor, after three generations of significant non-white migration, is the idea of multi-ethnicity and multiculturalism universally accepted. Britain is a civic nation, which thinks of itself still as an ethnic nation. There is a gulf between how it conceives of itself, in ethnic terms, and how it actually is. This gulf produces everything from bemused confusion to active resentment among everyone who cannot recognise their own place in the ethnic mythologies of the place. I mean not only 'visible' non-white minorities, but also the European and white Commonwealth immigrants who cannot identify with the ethnic story of Englishness. Nor is the gulf between what this country actually is and what it proclaims itself to be evident only to minorities and migrants. The widespread public support for constitutional reform is driven by a conviction not merely that the constitution should be both more just and more efficient, but that it should represent the people as they are. The reality is that what holds Britain together as a nation-state, what makes the place 'governable' in the thin version of national cohesion which I have offered, is no longer common tradition, national story, shared ethnicity, food and culture, but common language and common attachment to certain rules of the game. These rules need to be explicit: their enforcement should be strict, and the legitimacy of national institutions should be judged by the degree to which they both enforce the rules on citizens and live by them themselves. But this is a civic contract: the legitimacy of the rules – democracy, accountability, rule of law, procedural fairness, opportunity for all – depends on their fairness, not on their rootedness in a myth of common origins. Britain's nationalism remains ethnic, when in fact the social contract which keeps it governable is civic. Until its nationalism becomes truly civic, it cannot be benign.

NOTES ON CHAPTER 12

1 Michael Ignatieff is a well-known broadcaster and author of many books, including *Blood and Belonging* (London: BBC Books and Chatto and Windus, 1993); *Isaiah Berlin: A Life* (London: Chatto & Windus, 1998); *The Warrior's Honour: Ethnic War and the Modern Conscience* (London: Chatto & Windus, 1998).
2 Michael Ignatieff, *Blood and Belonging*, *op. cit.*
3 Robert Fine, 'The 'new nationalism' and democracy: a critique of pro patria', *Democratisation*, 1, 3, Autumn 1994.

13

BENIGN NATIONALISM? THE LIMITS OF THE CIVIC IDEAL

Robert Fine[1]

The idea of a 'benign nationalism' is an emergent theme within contemporary social theory. It goes under the name of 'civic nationalism', or 'national identity', or 'constitutional patriotism', or even 'post-nationalism'. It presents itself to the world as enlightened, tolerant, reflective, inclusive and rights-based. It prides itself on a realism which recognises the heterogeneity of nation-state – the mixed and hybrid populations they contain – as well as their necessity. It maintains, in the words of Michael Ignatieff, that a nation should be composed of 'all those – regardless of race, colour, creed, gender, language or ethnicity – who subscribe to the nation's political creed'. It visualises 'a community of equal, rights-bearing citizens, united in patriotic attachment to a shared set of political practices and values'.[2] It celebrates plurality and difference within the framework of the nation as a whole.

This new nationalism repudiates conventional nationalisms based on ethnic homogeneity, racial purity, blood, destiny or language, and indeed sees itself as providing the only reliable antidote to ethnic nationalism. Its core belief is, again to quote Michael Ignatieff, that 'the only guarantee that ethnic groups will live side by side in peace is shared loyalty to a state, strong enough, fair enough, equitable enough to command their obedience'.[3] From this perspective, what is wrong with the world is not nationalism itself, for every people hungers for a home, but rather the wrong kind of nationalism. The new nationalism accordingly reformulates the key struggle of our age as one between those who believe that a nation should be a home to all, and that race, colour, religion and creed should be no bar to belonging, and those who want their nation to be home only to 'their own'.

The new nationalism is opposed to the legacy of Marxism and the doctrine of internationalism. The link it sees between Marxism and the rise of ethnicity may be captured through an image drawn by the late Sir Isaiah Berlin, when he used the metaphor of a bent twig 'forced down so severely that, when it is released, it lashes back with fury'.[4] The basic argument is that when national sentiment is suppressed, as it is by Marxism and other forms of internationalism, a backlash comes with the irrepressible force that has been witnessed in some former outposts of the Russian empire. Internationalism and cosmopolitanism appear as the sign under which the plurality of national cultures is denied and a homogeneous image of global order is imposed in its place. In central Asia there was a modification of this pattern when reaction to the collapse of the Soviet empire involved appeals to previously suppressed Islamic transnationalisms.

Anti-ethnic and anti-Marxist, the new civic nationalism has caught the imagination of many intellectuals from many different countries and traditions. Its response to the collapse of communism on the one side and rise of ethnic nationalism and religious fundamentalism on the other affirms the interest of every citizen in respecting the authority of civic states in exchange for the state's respect for the rights of its citizens. In this sense, it has made patriotism once again an acceptable term within the liberal-left intelligentsia after many years of neglect, scepticism or downright hostility.

The new nationalism is a contemporary doctrine situated within our own age, but it wears the clothes of a former age, especially of the eighteenth century. It appeals to Montesquieu, Kant, Adam Smith and Herder who, it seems, knew something about how to combine civic patriotism with cosmopolitanism, national pride with respect for other nations, and national belonging with individual rights and freedoms. Enlightenment, romanticism and empiricism provide the styles of dress in which the new nationalism enters the public arena – as well as the possibility of family rows between rival national traditions. For French enlightenment thinkers Montesquieu is the hero and

Herder the villain.[5] Within Anglo-Saxon empiricism civic nationalism appears as a peculiarly British invention – based on shared attachment to the crown, parliament and the rule of law – which was successfully exported to other Western countries, except Germany, where a concept of nationhood defined in terms of the people's ethnic characteristics began its 'long and troubling career in European thought'.[6] For German romanticists, Herder is the hero (often contrasted with Fichte) and the so-called enlightened 'universalists' are the villain.[7] Small rivalries over which nation provides the ideal model for civic nationalism – France, Germany or Britain – do not obscure the common thread running through them: a return to a moment before the idea of an enlightened, tolerant, pluralistic and rights-respecting nation was corrupted by ethnicity on one side and internationalism on the other.

THE OPPOSITION BETWEEN THE CIVIC AND THE ETHNIC

Against the postulate of the new nationalism, that there is a fundamental opposition between civic and ethnic conceptions of the nation, I want to suggest that there is not only slippage from one to the other, but also displacement of the deficiencies of one onto the other. The watertight divide which civic nationalism sometimes attempts to construct between itself and ethnic nationalism turns out to be rather leaky.

From the point of view of civic nationalism, ethnic nationalism appears irrational, even pathological, as if the relation between them were one of light against darkness, reason against madness, tolerance against bigotry, freedom against authoritarianism etc. Julia Kristeva, for example, analyses the rise of ethnic nationalism in psychoanalytic mode as the work of wounded souls who move from defensive hatred to persecuting hatred, making others the scapegoat of their own depression and suppressed conflicts.[8] Michael Ignatieff ascribes the re-emergence of ethnic nationalism to a long-term crisis of national pride. But there is more to what is called 'ethnic nationalism' than this.

Hannah Arendt said in regard to her wartime commitment to Zionism something that we can all understand: that 'if one is attacked as a Jew, one must defend oneself as a Jew'.[9] Is this 'ethnic nationalism'? The same can be said about the nationalism of other oppressed peoples: Africans, Catalans, Armenians, Indians, Irish etc. The 'we' that resists is here the 'us' that has been abused. What is called 'ethnic nationalism' may be a battle cry in the face of injustice, and may offer its members a sense of humanity in an otherwise inhuman world. As Arendt put it, 'people cling to their nationality all the more desperately when they have lost the rights and protection that such nationality once gave them'.[10]

The danger arising from this 'ethnic' response to exclusion is that it will mirror the inhumanity, violence and racism of those who excluded them. In Central Europe demand for national self-determination has led twice in this century both to bitter national rivalries and to the growth within political communities of internal divisions between 'state peoples', 'minorities' and 'stateless peoples' – the latter having no government to represent them, and thereby losing the very right to have rights. On the other hand, however, if the category of 'ethnic nationalism' is defined broadly as that which is not 'civic', and becomes a term of abuse given by civic nationalists to all those who are responding in kind to earlier indignities, then the sense of resistance which can give meaning to ethnic nationalism has no visible presence and can become a repository for the guilt and implication of others. At least 'ethnic nationalism' faces up to the negativity of the existing world.

The basic difference between 'ethnic' and 'civic' forms of nationalism is that in the latter case it is the state which defines the nation, while in the former it is the nation which defines the state. The latter may provide a recipe for ethnic exclusivity but this distinction can also point to the radicalism of 'ethnic nationalism' and conservatism of 'civic nationalism' in relation to existing states. It is not surprising that people who are deprived of rights by existing states become convinced that their freedom can only be attained with the establishment of their 'own' government. The modern pariah – refugees and displaced persons who have no state – become the visible evidence that belonging to a nation which does have its own state is the condition of possessing those rights which enlightenment purports to grant to every individual by virtue of his or her humanity.

From the perspective of civic nationalism, ethnic nationalism is a madness which can only be explained psychologically; but from the perspective of ethnic nationalism, civic nationalism may appear as an oppressive doctrine of privilege which forgets its own origins. It forgets that in most European countries we have experienced slippages of 'civic' into 'ethnic' nationalism – particularly in the age of imperialism, when ideas of nationhood became infused with concepts of racial, religious and linguistic purity. It forgets that the ethnic nationalism of oppressed peoples often only mimics the racialised nationalism of the colonial powers. It forgets the violence, internal and external, that goes into the formation and perpetuation of the 'civic' nation-state. And it forgets how much more violence infuses civic nationalism when it becomes a principle of unlimited, self-expanding power.

From the perspective of ethnic nationalism, civic nationalism too often appears as a conservative ideology which demands the loyalty of everyone to the existing order of nation-states, offers no solution to the stateless except to go 'home', and is only too ready to label those who reject this order as bigots.

Thus, in the dualism of 'civic' versus 'ethnic' nationalism, the latter appears to the former as backward, but the former appears to the latter as the bearer of a new 'orientalism'.[11] To be sure, civic nationalists would wish to distinguish between their own ideals and the historical practices of the states which embody them, but can we simply go back to a civic idea of the nation as if the intervening history – including imperialism and its consequences – were merely an aberration to be rectified by taking, as Hannah Arendt put it, 'that which was good in the past and calling it our heritage, and by discarding that which was bad and thinking of it as a dead load which time will bury in oblivion'.[12] The conclusion I would draw is not to sanitise our own history under the register of civic nationalism but open our eyes to the fact that 'we', the children of Enlightenment, are closer to 'them', the ethnic cleansers, than we would like to think. 'We' were implicated in what Arendt called 'the decline of the nation-state', when Western states became imperial powers, established structures and ideas of racial exclusion at home and abroad, and somctimes inconsistently supported a 'right of national self-determination' which was used to underwrite the rise of 'ethnic nationalism' elsewhere.[13]

I put this argument not to support any light-minded relativism, as if there is nothing to choose between civic and ethnic nationalisms, still less a generalised cynicism, but rather to provoke a more troubling conclusion than the doctrine of civic nationalism contemplates: one which challenges our 'own' innocence. My argument is that civic nationalism not only observes but also surrenders to the fact that membership of a nation-state is the precondition of the right to have rights, and that rightlessness is the fate of those who have no nation-state. Like ancient Greeks, its protagonists conclude that their particular interests are preserved in the interest of the *polis* and they become patriots for fear of the barbarism beyond the city gates. In the modern world, however, it seems to me that their attachment of rights to the *polis* is a dangerous principle – not only for the excluded, but for all whose rights become dependent on the state. What is given with one hand can be taken away with the other.

There is another conclusion possible: that nationalism in all its forms is a danger to human rights, and that the right to have rights must be guaranteed by humanity itself.[14] I take my cue from this line of thought.

NATIONALISM IN GENERAL

The difference between civic and ethnic nationalism means that they are both forms of nationalism. To understand their difference we need also to comprehend their identity. Nationalism is a modern political doctrine which emerged in the aftermath of the French Revolution. Its basic principle is to uphold the national interest or national identity over all other interests and identities as the ultimate ground on which political judgement is based. The doctrine necessarily looks two ways: on the one side, it elevates the nation over the individual, declaring that, if necessary, it will sacrifice private interests and identities to the national good; on the other side it puts the interests of the nation before those of humanity as a whole or any larger international entity. First the nation, then your personal concerns; first the nation, then the interests of humanity – this is nationalism's order of priorities.

Can nationalism ever provide a good or valid criterion for action? We may fight for justice, or for equality, or for an end to poverty, or for freedom from colonial rule, or for human rights, or for an ecologically sound planet, but elevating the nation as such as a supreme value – and this is what making an 'ism' out of the nation does – surrenders our judgement to something which may be a force for freedom, democracy and culture one day but for terror, conquest and xenophobia the next. Nationalism is a fickle beast. In its best moods it liberates human beings from colonial oppression and unites people previously fragmented, but it also excludes those deemed not to belong and demands the active assent of its 'own' nationals. It attracts us through images of home, hearth, warmth and love, but it displaces emotions which belong to our personal lives onto political life, and thereby robs both of their value. As the former West German President, Gustav Heinemann, once said: 'I love my wife, not my country'.

Nationalism promises a touch of humanity in an inhuman world, but at the cost of what Hannah Arendt called a 'worldlessness', whereby humanity retreats behind the walls of the nation and clings to nationality as the foundation of its rights and security. Such humanity is dearly bought. It purports to put idealism before particular material interests, but its subordination of many voices to the one voice of the nation or to the singular will of the people lends itself to the prioritising of one interest over all others. It celebrates the plurality of nations over totalising conceptions of global reason, but without confronting the consequences of this form of pluralism. As Kant once put it,

> each nation sees its own majesty... in not having to submit to any external legal constraint, and the glory of its ruler consists in his power to order thousands of people to immolate themselves for a

> cause which does not truly concern them, while he need not himself incur any danger whatsoever.[15]

Nationalism is a fact of the modern world which cannot simply be willed away, but its claim to be either a natural or rational expression of political modernity serves only to invalidate other political arguments.

Ernest Gellner laid open the core nationalist myth that nations are a natural or rational way of classifying people.[16] He argued that if nationalism is a political principle which holds that the political and national unit should be congruent, it is logically possible that it could be impartial, pacifist, sweetly reasonable, but it is unlikely – not least because there are more potential nations on earth than viable states which could satisfy their aspirations. I think that Gellner was right, but I cannot accept his conclusion that, while intellectuals comprehend that nationalism is mythic, the people need such myths and that nationalism is our modern fate. Nationalism has a more chequered history than this image allows: it rises and falls, it is always in conflict with other political views, its particular brand of mythic violence may be as troubling for the 'people' as it is for the 'elite', it can serve a noble cause, but this does not mean that in itself it can ever provide a valid criterion for action. I would rather resume the search, which is as old as nationalism itself, for more genuine universals and a less violent pluralism.

MARXISM AND INTERNATIONALISM

The new nationalism rejects Marxist, liberal and other 'internationalist' critiques of nationalism on the grounds that they fail to understand the imperatives of national identity. They are said at best to ignore the need which individuals have for a sense of belonging, and at worst to suppress all manifestations of national belonging. In practice, however, at least in the post-war period, Marxism has been characterised not so much by 'anti-nationalism' as by, on the one hand, an extreme national chauvinism on behalf of the 'mother country' of communism, Russia, and on the other by an assimilation to certain kinds of 'Third World' nationalism; all this in the name, but only the name, of 'internationalism'. Many anti-colonial nationalist movements have utilised justifications of a Marxist kind, and actually existing Marxism, even when it denounces particular anti-colonial nationalist movements and regimes, and yet have not given any less priority to national liberation struggles. Socialism was often seen through a basically nationalist lens: as Eric Hobsbawm and Benedict Anderson have both observed, though from different viewpoints, the proclivity of post-war Marxism has been to 'swallow nationalist assumptions whole'.[17]

The idea of two nationalisms, one basically good and the other bad, was originally a Marxist doctrine which made a certain sense at the time of its formulation – when the world was divided between colonisers and colonised – but increasingly turned into an arbitrary distinction closely related to Russian foreign policy interests. The 'nationalism of the oppressed' became that nationalism which allied itself to Russia in the Cold War. Internationalism got a very bad name when it became the disguise under which the Soviet government justified all manner of imperialist expansions of its own. Just as the name of 'cosmopolitanism' turned sour after the French revolution, when it was used to justify French imperial conquests, so too the name 'internationalism' turned sour after the Russian revolution when used to justify the subordination of all other national interests to those of Russia. In both cases, the idea of a 'universal nation' – a nation whose particular interests are identified with the universal interests of humanity as a whole – extinguishes all dreams of a genuinely cosmopolitan order. If 'Marxism' was a factor in the growth of ethnic nationalism, it was not in the manner of Isaiah Berlin's 'bent twig', but because the real content of official and often unofficial Marxism was thoroughly nationalistic. This is perhaps one reason why 'cosmopolitanism' was employed as a term of abuse which Stalinists threw at Jewish and other dissenters.

ENLIGHTENMENT AND COSMOPOLITANISM

There was a current within Enlightenment thought that prioritised the interests of 'humanity' over those of the nation. In France Montesquieu put this position with famous eloquence when he wrote:

> If I knew something useful to my homeland and detrimental to Europe and to Humankind, I would consider it a crime... All *particular* duties cease when they cannot be accomplished without offending *human* duties... The duty of a citizen is a crime when it leads one to forget the duty of *man*...[18]

In Germany, Kant looked to a time when war would eventually lead states to abandon their 'lawless state of savagery' and enter a federation of peoples in which every state, even the smallest, could expect to derive its security and rights 'not from its own power... but solely from this united power and the law-governed decisions of a united will'.[19] Wars between nations, he believed, would eventually compel humanity to overcome narrow definitions of national self-interest, introduce a 'universal cosmopolitan existence', and enforce cosmopolitan law upon nations.

What did Kant mean by this term 'universal cosmopolitan existence'? A federation of free states whose aim was to secure peace by common agreement but which would not be equated with the interests of a single global power. International laws which prevent one state from forcibly interfering in the constitution and government of another. Laws of 'universal hospitality' which grant strangers the right to be treated with civility when they arrive on someone else's territory, and which prevent states from treating newly-acquired territories as 'ownerless' and their native inhabitants 'as nothing'. Laws which prohibit what are now called 'war crimes', 'crimes against peace' and 'crimes against humanity'. Most of all, universal cosmopolitan existence requires a recognition that the peoples of the earth have, as he put it, 'entered in varying degrees into a universal community where a violation of rights in one part of the world is felt everywhere'.[20]

This is a less 'totalising' image of cosmopolitanism than any recipe for imposing singular, homogenising norms over a plurality of national cultures. Kant's optimism that the spread of republicanism and commerce would make possible this 'universal cosmopolitan existence' was certainly misplaced, but his cosmopolitan convictions – in favour of overcoming national parochialism in all its forms – expressed the universal spirit of Enlightenment as much as any appeal to civic nationalism. This spirit was present in the early stages of the French Revolution, when the 'sovereignty of the nation' expressed in the Declaration of the Rights of Man and Citizen indicated the struggle against absolutism and birth of popular sovereignty, rather than French nationalism. As Kristeva reminds us, for a brief period during the French Revolution there was a notable lack of nationalist sentiment. Decrees were passed offering French citizenship to all foreigners who had resided in France for five years and had some means of subsistence; societies and newspapers for foreigners were encouraged; the use of force against other nations was disavowed; support was given to revolutionaries from other countries to rid themselves of their own absolutist rulers; and certain 'benefactors of mankind' – including Tom Paine, Mary Wollstonecraft, William Wilberforce and even Jeremy Bentham – were awarded honorary French citizenship.[21] To be sure, this new dawn did not last. As revolutionary wars were launched in the name of the universal nation, so too xenophobia became an internal political force. Foreigners were held responsible for whatever went wrong: military defeats, economic problems, political crises. The clubs and newspapers of foreigners were disbanded. Even Tom Paine, 'citizen of the world', the man who signed himself 'Humanus', was imprisoned and eventually expelled. When revolutionary terror was directed at those deemed to put their particular interests before the people, it was aimed especially at foreigners.

CIVIC NATIONALISM AND SOCIAL INEQUALITY

Civic nationalism stands for a liberal-democratic state based on popular sovereignty which inwardly respects the rights of individuals and associations of civil society and outwardly develops co-operative and friendly relations with other nations. Why, then, is it necessary to assert this kind of nationalist or patriotic attachment? Why assume that such an argument is needed, and that liberal democracy by itself is insufficient?

One answer is that the cold rationality of liberal contractarianism is not enough: we are emotional as well as rational beings, and the stirrings of the flag, the anthem, the military parade, the pomp and ceremony of the nation, are as important for solidarity as any utilitarian calculus. By itself, it seems, liberalism is too rational, too bloodless, too cold. Emotions are certainly a vital part of any analysis of nationalism, and more widely of politics in general, but what place should they have in our understanding of common membership in constituted polities? The 'emotional' is not the only thing we can talk about when trying to go beyond 'the rational' – we are also symbolic, imaginative, poetic and metaphorical beings – but in any case it is a dangerous principle to place feeling and enthusiasm rather than reason at the heart of our political commitments.

The idea of civic nationalism points to the insufficiency of liberal democracy, and is invoked when rational self-interest and commitment to liberal values do not suffice. I would suggest, then, that the re-emergence of civic nationalism is not only a response to the fall of communism and rise of ethnic nationalism, but also to the pressures currently placed on liberal democracy both by disintegrative political forces and by social factors such as unemployment and poverty. The idea of civic nationalism offers in this context an emotive source of political cohesion and the hope that a 'strong but equitable' state will keep ethnic violence at bay. This is the source of its strength as an idea. But it also engenders faith in the state rather than critical reflection, and a sidelining of social questions rather than a determination to tackle them. In the name of nation building, it may tell workers not to strike, activists not to mobilise, the disaffected not to riot and the unemployed to look harder for work. In matters of foreign policy it may speak the language of 'national interest' over all wider concerns. To ethnic minorities it may demand allegiance to the existing nation-state as a precondition for acceptance. Finally, to resurgent conservative nationalism it offers a more enlightened alternative, but its instinct is to concede ground.

Civic nationalism appears benign to the extent that it acts as an antidote to the dangers of both ethnic nationalism and a so-called 'internationalism' that refuses all forms of nationalism except its own. It is not, however, the only antidote on offer, and among its side-effects I would include the following: it confronts 'ethnic nationalism' on the latter's own nationalistic ground; it utilises the term 'ethnic nationalism' ideologically as its other; it downplays supra-national solidarities in favour of a certain kind of patriotism; it subsumes social reform to national unity; and it promotes faith in the state rather than a critical and reflective political culture. At bottom, civic and ethnic forms of nationalism are not so alien from one another as they at first sight appear: there is kinship between a politics based on patriotism and what Rorty has called the 'politics of difference', based on internal divisions within the nation.[22] Not only does the bifurcation of nationalism into benign and malign enemy camps – whether on the basis of the old substantive distinction between the nationalism of the oppressors and the oppressed, or on the basis of the new formal distinctions between ethnic and civic nationalism – deny the equivocation which runs through nationalism itself, but its moral division of the world between 'them' and 'us' robs the world of all political profundity.

Excluded from this opposition are the speculative possibilities manifested especially in the breaks, warps and distortions of our political experience. In thinking about such possibilities – those which Walter Benjamin termed the 'immanent absolute' of our political experience[23] – we should avoid the trap of now devaluing nationalism absolutely, as if it no longer has any normative or ethical content whatsoever. Such reactive inversion of nationalist sentiment does not take us much further in our understanding of what nationalism is. In addition, it tends to pathologise nationalism as the folly of others, and thus not to recognise it in oneself.[24]

If one pitfall lies in the absolute devaluation of nationalism, another related pitfall may lie in the absolute overvaluation of cosmopolitanism.[25] This is the beginning of another story, but we cannot assume that cosmopolitanism – however conceived – is free from the equivocations which unsettle nationalism. Cosmopolitanism is not a miraculous physic and cannot be above the contradictions of our political world. It certainly attracts me (and many others) more than any nationalist credo – not least because it has been a name of abuse aimed at the homeless pariah who is refused, or refuses, participation in national communities, and also because 'homelessness' now increasingly appears as our contemporary fate. Yet the history of 'internationalism', that it was put into the service of a great power and used by it to crush little powers, should make us hesitate to put our faith in cosmopolitanism as its 'purer' predecessor and possible heir. The movement from 'internationalism' to 'cosmopolitanism' symbolises the need to escape from a sullied past, to turn 'universality' and 'humanity' from abstract ideas observed only in their violation into an actual presence, and to identify with the victims. But faith in the *cosmopolis*, no less than faith in the *polis*, conceals the violence of its own abstraction and raises its own equivocations. After all, it could be said that the contemporary peripatetic corporate capitalist is one role model for cosmopolitanism, or that totalitarian regimes persecuted Jews because they saw in 'Jewish cosmopolitanism' a rival to their own supra-national ambitions. Cosmopolitanism has the great virtue of making us think about the limits of every form of nationalism, but what is needed is a less transcendent understanding of the possibilities immanent within modern political life. We could at least make it a rule of thumb for present-day politics that we cannot escape equivocation, contradiction, ambiguity, anxiety etc wherever we look – either through the discovery of a new concept or the rediscovery of an old.

NOTES ON CHAPTER 13

1 Robert Fine is a reader in Sociology and Co-Director of the Centre for Social Theory at the University of Warwick. Among other publications, he is author of *Democracy and the Rule of Law* (London: Pluto, 1985); *Beyond Apartheid: Nation and Class in South Africa* (London: Pluto, 1990); *Being Stalked* (London: Chatto and Windus, 1998). His *After the Revolution: the Politics of Hegel, Marx and Arendt* will be published by UCL/Routledge in 2000. This article is based on a debate held with Michael Ignatieff at the University of Warwick, and pursues arguments first aired in Robert Fine, 'The new nationalism and democracy: a critique of pro patria', *Democratisation* 1/3, Autumn 1994.

2 Michael Ignatieff, *Blood and Belonging* (London: BBC Books and Chatto and Windus, 1993), p 3.

3 *Ibid.*, p 185.

4 Isaiah Berlin, 'Two concepts of nationalism', *New York Review of Books* (interview with Nathan Gardels), pp 19–23, 21 November 1991.

5 See, for example, Julia Kristeva, *Nations without Nationalism* (New York: Columbia University Press, 1993).

6 Ignatieff, *Blood and Belonging*, *op. cit.*, p 4.

7 Berlin, 'Two concepts of nationalism', *op. cit.*

8 Kristeva, *Nations without Nationalism*, *op. cit.*

9 Hannah Arendt, *Essays in Understanding 1930–1954* (London: Harcourt Brace and Co., 1994), p.12.
10 *Ead.*, *The Origins of Totalitarianism* (Andre Deutsch, London, 1986), p 300.
11 Edward Said, *Orientalism* (Harmondsworth: Penguin, 1985).
12 The imagery comes from Arendt, *Totalitarianism*, *op. cit.*, Preface, p viii.
13 Arendt, *Totalitarianism*, *op. cit.*, ch. 9.
14 Arendt, *Totalitarianism*, *op. cit.*, ch. 9.
15 Emmanuel Kant, *Kant's Political Writings*, (ed. Hans Reiss) (Cambridge: Cambridge University Press, 1984), p 103.
16 Ernest Gellner, *Nations and Nationalism* (Oxford: Blackwell, 1990).
17 Benedict Anderson, *Imagined Communities: Reflections on the Origin and Spread of Nationalism* (London: Verso, 1990); Eric Hobsbawm, 'Some reflections on the Break-up of Britain' in *Politics for a Rational Left* (London: Verso, 1989), p 140.
18 Quoted in Julia Kristeva, *Strangers to Ourselves* (New York: Columbia University Press, 1991), p 131.
19 Kant, *Political Writings*, *op. cit.*, p 47.
20 Kant, *Political Writings*, *op. cit.*, pp 107–8.
21 Kristeva, *Strangers to Ourselves*, *op. cit.*, pp 154–7.
22 See Martha Nussbaum, 'Patriotism and Cosmopolitanism', *Boston Review* vol. XIX, no. 5, Oct/Nov 1994 and M. Billig, 'Nationalism and Richard Rorty', *New Left Review* 202, Nov-Dec 1993.
23 See Howard Caygill, *Walter Benjamin: The Colour of Experience* (London: Routledge, 1998), ch. 1.
24 I think that this is a problem which Jürgen Habermas gets himself into when he declares in the name of a post-metaphysical concept of the political that whatever value it had in the past in the pursuit of anti-colonial struggles and in the building of welfare states, 'nationalism', normatively speaking, 'is now dead', and in the same breath declares that 'constitutional patriotism' is alive and well. See Habermas, *Between Facts and Norms* (Cambridge: Polity, 1997), Appendices 1 and 2.
25 See, for example, the defence of cosmopolitanism in Martha Nussbaum's contribution to M.C. Nussbaum and J. Cohen (eds), *For Love of Country: Debating the Limits of Patriotism* (Boston: Beacon Press, 1996). She argues that in the battles between civic and ethnic forms of nationalism, as they have been waged in the USA, 'what we share as both rational and mutually dependent human beings was simply not on the agenda'. This is a crucial point to make, but it does not follow that we should therefore identify this sense of common humanity with the particular doctrine of 'cosmopolitanism'.

INDEX